THINK IT.
DO IT!

*Lessons from Visionaries
Who Brought Their Ideas to Life*

DR. DIANE J. HINDS

ISBN: 0990659062
ISBN: 13: 9780990659068

Library of Congress Control Number: 2014913683
Achieve Publishing
St Paul, MN

Diane Hinds, Ed.D.
PO Box 120601
New Brighton, MN 55112
www.achieveandsucceed.net

ACKNOWLEDGEMENTS

This book began as my dissertation. After completing that academic undertaking, I was excited by what I learned and wanted to share it in a more readable and practical form. Dissertations are notorious for being heavy on academic and light on readability. In an effort to make what I'd written for academics more accessible to anyone and everyone, I started on the adventure to create something new—this book!

In doing the research reported in my dissertation, I found that individuals who are successful in taking their ideas from conception to implementation involve other people. My own experience in bringing this book to life validates this finding and I want to acknowledge the help and support I have received.

My thanks to my advisors, instructors and colleagues from the Organization Development doctorate program at the University of St. Thomas, including, Mitch Kusy, Diane Stoy, John Conbere, Sharon Gibson, Raj Bekee, Marney Halligan, Karen Keenan, and Colleen Stevens. Thanks also to Richard Brynteson from Concordia University, who served as one of my dissertation advisors.

I thank my friends who helped me throughout this journey: Kay Kovach, Bob Sater, Lisa Stock, Jeffrey Cookson, Joe Spartz, Mike Driscoll, Fran Kieselhorst, Joan Zwach, Naomi Beckering, Jan Bosch, Mary Nosek, Pat McHugo, and Judy McHugo. My thanks to Cynthia Tague and my daughter Karen Hinds for the many hours they spent transcribing the tapes of my interviews.

I also want to thank the participants in this study for sharing their experiences with me. Their accomplishments are inspiring and I am pleased that this project brought me into contact with such outstanding individuals.

As with all aspects of my life, I owe so much to my husband, Tom Hinds, who has been by my side throughout the whole process, and to my children, Mark and Karen Hinds and the other member of our family, Lisl Fuhrken. They are my source of joy and it is to them that I dedicate this work.

TABLE OF CONTENTS

*Every great dream begins
with a dreamer.
Always remember that you
have within you
the strength, the patience,
and the passion
to reach for the stars
to change the world.*

Harriet Tubman

1

Introduction

▲

Ever have a **GREAT** idea that just bubbles up in your mind like a volcano? You rush to share your idea with a friend. You have all the enthusiasm of a young child splashing in the ocean for the first time. The idea is so great you're ready to abandon your day job and jump into this new adventure. But the challenges of bringing your idea to life dampen your enthusiasm. The idea retreats to a dark corner of your mind, only to surface during other flights of fancy. If this is your experience, you are not alone.

Many people fantasize about creating something new but never move beyond the dreaming stage. Having the dream is an important part of the process, but much more than just being a dreamer is required to bring an idea to reality. Some people engage in conversations with others about their ideas, but for many that is where it stops. They don't move beyond the conversations. They talk about a compelling need for their product or service, or how wonderful it would be if the idea materialized, and yet talk evaporates into inaction and nothing is done. As one executive stated, *"We're great at talking. We talk about new ideas all the time. We have more ideas than we can handle. Our trouble is in making something happen"* (J. Spartz).

Individuals often start to bring their ideas to life by completing the easiest or most obvious steps, only to abandon the work when the first obstacle appears. Most people are content staying on the familiar path. Stephen Covey, author of one of the most popular business books of all time, *Seven Habits of Highly Effective People*, (2004) stated that most people can see opportunities for advancement or improvement in a situation, but many of them fail to take the necessary steps to make it happen.

Even with all the obvious benefits of achieving one's dream, people often talk themselves out of pursuing it. Our fears come to the forefront, and our brilliant ideas often never leave the starting gate. We find excuses for inaction, frequently looking for reasons outside ourselves. Sometimes, upon reflection, we may acknowledge our own inadequacies and bemoan our lack of follow through. And we have lots of company who are doing the same thing.

Failure to implement ideas is a common topic at business meetings and hallway discussions in many organizations. Learning how to execute has become a popular workshop topic at conferences. In addition, in my professional experience, I encounter numerous individuals and organizations who are seeking to generate new ideas and implement them. However, few are successful. There are many great ideas that never make it out of the board room or off the planning document. Many individuals dream their dreams without being able to, or choosing not to take action to realize their idea.

Wanting, hypothesizing, planning, and making initial attempts are not enough to bring an idea into reality. Many people take the important and difficult first step of identifying what they want to accomplish, but they get stuck trying to implement their ideas. Planning and processes, no matter how comprehensive, won't guarantee action. A professional coach, who is a participant in this study, noted that a significant portion of his work is due to an individual having an idea but needing help to bring it to fruition. *"The majority of self-help books are written precisely because it is difficult to realize one's dreams"* (J. Earley). Not only do individuals have difficulty bringing their ideas to fruition, but groups, teams, and organizations as well, frequently struggle with successfully implementing their ideas.

Many people think about creating something new, but few actually fulfill such a dream. They settle for what life hands them instead of creating the extraordinary future they desire. However, some people go beyond talking and thinking. They act. They overcome obstacles. They are not derailed by early defeat. When they experience failure, they accept it and use it as an accelerator to discover a new path that will lead them to other ways that will work. They put forth the effort to see their ideas through to fruition, unwilling to leave their dreams unrealized. They create something that did not exist before. Why are creative ideas just daydreams for most, but a call to action for others? The specific research questions included in this study are:

1. How do individuals who bring an idea to fruition initially develop their creative ideas?
2. What motivates individuals to take action to bring their ideas to life?
3. What processes or methods do individuals employ to move their ideas from concept to implementation?
4. What meaning do individuals who bring an idea from inception through implementation take from this experience?

5. What are the traits and characteristics of individuals who bring an idea to life?

This book explores answers to these questions and provides insight from those who have brought their ideas to life. Their stories can lay out a path for others who want to undertake the exciting and challenging journey of moving from an idea to a functioning reality.

Individuals who successfully bring their ideas to life gain from the experience of doing so. Lives full of experience and accomplishment are rewarding and satisfying. Striving to, and achieving a goal puts us in the best position to learn what life has to teach us. Deliberate focus on accomplishing a goal enables us to structure our actions to achieve that goal and gain the satisfaction of a job well done. Not only do the individuals who bring their ideas to life benefit from realizing their vision, but other individuals, groups, and society also benefit from these achievements.

Being one of those people who frequently has "**GREAT**" ideas, but little results, I was fascinated to learn how other people actually made the journey from idea to implementation. Part of the reason I chose this topic was because I couldn't find good resources to answer the questions of this study. There is limited data-driven research regarding how individuals who successfully implement their ideas move from idea inception to implementation, nor is there an understanding of the traits and characteristics of individuals who successfully fulfill their dreams. Much more is known about planning a strategy than is known about the actual doing and making strategy work. Research shows that most people think and plan about what they want to create and seldom get around to getting it done.

This book examines how individuals brought their ideas to life and identifies common themes of the phenomenon of taking an idea from inception to reality. The stories in this book serve as guides and inspiration for other people who want to pursue their own dreams. The wisdom shared by these visionaries can help individuals who seek to create something new gain insight as to the approach and processes that lead to success. In addition, knowing the characteristics and traits of those who successfully created something new may help employers, team leaders, and others identify individuals who are likely to be able to perform such tasks. Also, individuals who wish to see their ideas realized may be able to determine which characteristics or traits they want to develop in themselves, or find in others, to help them implement their ideas.

The precise definition of *bringing an idea to life* is somewhat unique for each participant in the study, and reflects the distinctive elements of the individuals' stories. However, each of the participants shares the common experience of making an idea they formulated come into being. The ideas involved the thought to create something outside of one's self. They are not the accomplishment of a personal goal, such as becoming physically fit or climbing a mountain. Nor are they instantaneous or heroic acts, such as jumping into a swirling river to save someone who is drowning. The achievements studied in this book are the result of intentional action. The participants purposefully created something to be enduring and sustainable. The accomplishment of the idea resulted in the creation of something concrete and tangible.

The original seed of the idea may have come from the desire for something abstract. But at some point in the process, the idea became something concrete. For example, the first stirrings of an idea may be an abstract aspiration to eliminate world hunger but, for this study, the idea explored would be the development of a specific organization or a program that addresses some aspect of eradicating world hunger.

There is intrinsic value in telling the stories of people who have moved from idea to action. We learn a great deal from knowing others' stories. You'll be introduced to these amazing people and the entities they created in Chapter 2.

Chapters 3 – 8 explore the common themes that emerged from an analysis of the data gathered from these individuals and their stories. Chapter 9 discusses how these individuals define their experience. Chapter 10 is a closing discussion, followed by an Appendix that provides a description of the research methodology of this study.

Throughout the book you'll find worksheets that can help you create your own process for bringing your ideas to life. It is a challenging journey, but well worth the effort!

Doing the research for this book was an informative adventure for me and I am pleased to share with you what I discovered.

2

Visionaries and the Ideas
They Brought to Life

▲

When I selected this topic for my dissertation, one of my first tasks was to find individuals who had actually created something new—who had an idea and followed it through to fruition. This search proved to be extremely easy and rather fun. Some people were referred to me by friends and colleagues who knew my topic. Others, I found by myself by simply identifying an entity and asking, "I wonder whose idea this was?" Everyone I approached was interested in telling their story. My natural curiosity and their willingness to share their experiences with me made the interviewing process not only educational, but enjoyable as well.

Each story provides insights into the phenomenon of bringing an idea to life and about the traits and characteristics of the individuals who created something tangible and enduring. Following is a list of the individuals profiled in this book and the ideas they brought to life.

1. **Stan Appelbaum**, a retired businessman, developed Foster Care Council of Southwest Florida, which has changed its name to Friends of Foster Children, a non-profit organization that provides financial

assistance, tutoring, and support to children in the foster care system of Southwest Florida.

▲

2. **Jim Earley** left a successful career working in a large corporation to establish Trailblazer Coaching, an independent, single practitioner coaching practice.

▲

3. **Justin Griep** is a high-tech genius who created Cygentech, a business that helps organizations preparing for a public stock offering make their systems function effectively and provides other technical services to improve their business operations.

▲

4. **Christianna Hang** created Hmong College Prep Academy, a charter school specifically designed to serve the needs of Hmong students.

▲

5. **Sona Mehring** built a website to help friends communicate with their family and friends during a health crisis. This initial site morphed to become CaringBridge, an online caring community that has helped millions stay connected during medical and other life challenges.

▲

6. **Bernie Reisberg** developed his own manufacturing and importing company, Top Star, which creates and sells goods internationally. The name of the company was recently changed to East Asia Trade.

▲

7. **Sister Jean Thuerauf**, a Catholic nun, started Cookie Cart, a bakery located in an economically depressed area of Minneapolis, which provides not only great cookies, but also positive experiences and employment for at-risk youth.

▲

8. **Charlie and Maria Girsch,** a married couple who, after years of being successful toy inventors, developed a training and consulting business called Creativity Central.

▲

9. **Dr. Bill and Nancy Lascheid,** a married couple, both health care professionals, created the Neighborhood Health Clinic that serves the working poor in Naples, Florida.

▲

10.**Ken Miller and Jack Mannion** were instrumental in creating Water For People, an international organization that helps poor communities have a sustainable source of potable water and provides education on sanitation and hygiene.

▲

11.**Dick and Florence Nogaj,** a married couple, created Harvest for Humanity, a blueberry farm in Immokalee, Florida, which paid all workers a livable wage and Jubilation Housing Community that provides farm workers affordable housing and a sense of community.

Following are brief stories about these individuals and how they moved from conceiving an idea to bringing it to life.

STAN APPELBAUM
Foster Care Council of Southwest Florida
Friends of Foster Children
www.friendsoffosterchildren.net

Stan Appelbaum spent nearly his entire childhood in foster care. It was a difficult and challenging experience. Later in life, he decided to do something to help improve the lives of children in foster care. He developed a corporation that provides assistance to foster children in Southwest Florida.

Stan was placed in an orphanage when he was six months old. He lived in a variety of foster homes throughout his childhood. He explained that moving from home to home, a common experience for most foster children, was unsettling. He never really felt he belonged. Not all of the homes provided a caring, nurturing environment. In fact, some were abusive. In one home, when Stan was about seven years old, he slept in an unheated porch and wasn't allowed to eat with the family. Beatings were a regular ritual. At one point he was beaten so badly that he was hospitalized. He was moved from that home, only to have a series of placements that continued the abuse and neglect.

When he was about 10, he was sent to an orphanage. He stayed there for five years, and then was told to leave. He was given the choice of going to reform school, or taking $20 and heading out on his own. He took the $20. "I was kicked out of the orphanage at fifteen because I was a pretty angry guy." He left the system and chose to fend for himself in Hell's Kitchen, a notoriously rough neighborhood in New York City. There he saw a lot of other "thrown away" kids who turned to crime and some who seemed to barely exist. He wanted more. "I knew the only way to be in charge of my life was to take control of my life because frankly no one else did."

So at fifteen he made the decision that he was going to be successful. He was blessed with the intelligence and resiliency to make significant changes in his life. Stan got a job in construction and found a place to live with other orphanage alums. He was able to get financial help and went to school. Later, he served in the Korean War, married, had children, and over time became a successful businessman.

After retiring, Stan decided he wanted to do something to help the community. He was particularly interested in helping children. He had always participated in community activities, but the requirements of managing a business had demanded much of his time. He now felt he had the time to do something more substantial to help other people. Having been a foster child, he understood the harsh realities of that life and focused his attention on finding a way to help improve the lives of children in foster care.

He became a Guardian Ad Litem, whereby he was assigned as an advocate for specific children who were involved in the court system. He was later appointed to a human rights group by the Governor of Florida and served on several boards and committees, many of which concerned the welfare of children. Although these experiences were satisfying, Stan decided something more needed to be done to help children in foster care.

Looking back on his experience as a foster child and Guardian Ad Litem advocate for children, Stan observed,

> Children come into the system seriously damaged; could be physical abuse, neglect, sexual abuse and just the inability of parents to take care of them because they [the parents] are involved with drugs and alcohol. So the state, in its wisdom, sends a protective investigator out who interviews the family, looks over the situation and determines this child is in danger and is required to remove the child. The worker gives the family about five minutes to pack up whatever meager possessions the child has, which is usually put into a trash bag, and is carried out with the child or children with the protective investigator. Now I don't care what age you are, if you are an infant or eight or twelve or a teenager, you are going to be concerned by this treatment. This is how these children come into care.

Stan wanted to do something to enrich the lives of children who are brought in to such a system. He knew that even though there had been attempts to improve foster care, incidents of abuse and neglect were still common and most children in foster care felt a sense of insecurity.

Stan knew how difficult it was to change the governmental system that managed children's placement and care. He decided rather than trying to change this system, he would collaborate with the government to establish a council that would provide enrichment activities and special items for children in foster care. He brought together some close friends who shared his interest in serving children, and in 1999, they began the Foster Care Council of Southwest Florida. After a somewhat frustrating journey through the bureaucratic obstacle course required to secure approval for this council, the group's first need was to raise money. With connections throughout the community, they were able to raise more than adequate funds. They did several of the traditional fund raising activities, such as golf tournaments, grants, and entertainment programs. They also had innovative approaches to fund rising, such as raffles of McDonalds' stock, and an elaborate wine festival. Through hard work and dedication, the Foster Care Council was able to enrich the lives of several children in their first year of operation. Buoyed by their success in the first year, they set their sights on helping even more children in the next year, and they continue to challenge themselves and the community to do more for more children.

The name of the organization has changed to Friends of Foster Children of Southwest Florida (FFC) and it has experienced significant growth. In 2000, the organization was staffed by one part-time director and a handful of volunteers. In 2013, there were three full-time and one part-time staff and more than a hundred volunteers.

One of their primary services is to provide tutoring to help children overcome the educational lapses that occur due to frequent moving and changing schools. They also fund activities and items not provided by the government, including musical instruments, sports equipment, and participating in summer camp. Stan explained that these are the kind of things that "normal" children have and not having them is one of the factors that makes children in foster care feel "different." In addition, children are provided clothing for special occasions, such as the prom.

They have established a cooperative relationship with the government and are well supported by the community. Their "Boots and Boogie Bash," "Comedy Cabaret" and "Sip and Sample" fund raisers are popular events in the Southwest Florida area that provide a significant portion of FFC's financial support.

The FFC mission is *"To provide abused, neglected and abandoned children in Southwest Florida with the social, educational and financial support that state does not."* The organization continues to grow, and the services it provides to children are expanding. Stan has been recognized for his work with children, and recently received the "Friend for a Lifetime" award for his extraordinary volunteer contributions to benefit the lives of foster children. Stan is proud of what the group has been able to accomplish and continues to look for ways to improve the lives of children in foster care.

Words of Wisdom from Stan Appelbaum

- You have to be passionate; you need a goal.

- You have to have enough reason to do it so that it energizes you; encompasses all of your abilities to create something that is difficult to create.

- There may be people who are smarter than you, or have more advantages than you, but you will be successful if you are willing to put out the extra energy and effort that it takes to make it happen. It is hard work. Hard work wins out.

▲▲▲

Children enjoying some reading time with help from FFC

Stan Appelbaum,
founder of Friends of Foster Children.

JIM EARLEY
Trailblazer Coaching
www.trailblazercoaching.com

For many years, Jim Earley got up every morning and went to work. He was a good, responsible employee who did his job and got along well with other people. He had a gnawing sense that maybe there was something else out there for him, but being a stable, risk-adverse kind of guy, Jim stayed in this pattern. Not terribly upset, just not really happy about his work.

Then, in a relatively short period of time in the early '90s, everything changed. Jim recognized that his job, although secure and financially rewarding, didn't give him a sense of fulfillment and purpose. He felt compelled to think about doing something else. He described this feeling as a kind of a metaphysical awareness. He said it was a sense that what he was doing was not what he *should* be doing. He had no clue what he should be doing, but he knew that he was not where he belonged.

> So I went home from work one day with a profound sense of dissatisfaction and, in one of the little quirky miracles of life, I was enrolled in a seminar, and the topic of the seminar was

accomplishment. That night I went to my semi-nar, and we were talking about the nature of accomplishment. I saw crystal clear that I was never going to have any sense of accomplish-ment working at that company. And it had nothing to do with the company. It was just the wrong fit. It wasn't about the people, the indus-try, or anything else. It was just that I shouldn't be there.

Jim told a friend about his desire to have work that gave him a sense of purpose. This friend had done research about the true nature of courage and said that many people defined courage as facing something you were afraid of. However, he said that true courage was the willingness to face the truth and take the appropriate action to react to this truth. As long as we avoid really accepting the truth, we can convince ourselves to stay on a path that is comfortable and familiar. Once we actually recognize that the truth requires we go in a different direction, and we make that course adjustment, that is when we truly exhibit courage. Jim Earley courageously faced the truth that he was never going to experience a sense of accomplishment working where he was, and having a sense of accomplishment was important to him. Therefore, trusting that he would be able to create something meaningful, he quit his very stable and secure position to begin a journey of personal discovery. His goal was to find his life's work; to be able to make a living doing something he found fulfilling.

Jim knew that he was interested in people, specifically in helping people figure out how to address the problems they faced. He knew he was a good listener. People told him he was easy to talk to and that they appreciated his counsel. Jim searched to find a title or job description that fit what he was looking for and he settled on being a "coach." This happened in the early '90s before coaching, outside of sports, was a popular profession. His initial plan was to find an employer who would hire him to perform coaching, but it became obvious that if he wanted to pursue coaching, he would have to create his own business.

By nature, Jim is not a risk taker, but he left the security of the corporate world and launched a coaching practice. This new business was one that he saw not as a job, but as a calling. One major problem he faced was that he had no desire to create his own business. He didn't know how to go about starting a business and was rather intimidated by the prospect. However, the desire for work that provided a sense of purpose and fulfillment was stronger than his fear of entrepreneurship, and he began the process of creating his own business to provide coaching services.

He was surprised that he was even considering opening a business. It wasn't anything he ever thought he would do. At the time he told a friend, "I don't know how to be an entrepreneur; I don't know that I even know how to spell the word." Regardless of his early hesitation, he knew that to achieve his vision, he would have to become an entrepreneur, as scary and difficult to spell as that was.

The new adventure of creating his own business put Jim in situations he didn't think he would ever face. A friend invited him to attend a meeting where Jim would have the opportunity to present himself to a group of people and talk about his work as a coach. As uncomfortable as he was going to a meeting and talking before a group of total strangers, Jim realized that this was a great opportunity for him. As the meeting progressed and it got closer to the time for him to talk, he had to fight off his inclination to dash for the door.

And my little head just started smokin', as most of me was saying, "GO HOME!" But the part that had some wisdom said, "Go home if you want to, but how are you ever gonna find a client if you run home?" So, I took the microphone. I stood up, and I said something I really don't remember what, and I probably turned beet red. And the next day a guy called me and he said, "I heard you last night at the Minnesota Entrepreneurs' Club, and you're exactly what I'm looking for, and I didn't know I was looking for anything!" So we met and he hired me.

This first testing of the waters was pretty solid reinforcement that Jim was on the right track. He was encouraged that he was finding a way to bring his idea to life.

Working through his network of friends and associates, Jim was able to do what was necessary to set up a business and begin his coaching practice. It was not a straight path, but rather one that allowed him to explore alternatives and find the right choices for him. He doesn't always do everything the way that the business books advise, but he finds something that works for him and continues to grow and diversify his business.

His intention in setting up his coaching practice was to help others recognize and realize their potential. Most of Jim's clients are at the mid-career stage in their lives and are looking for ways to revitalize their careers. Like Jim, some clients are seeking significant changes in their life and work to achieve a greater sense of satisfaction. He helps them find their own paths and gently nudges them along to do what is needed to realize their goals. Jim's own story serves as example to his clients about the importance of figuring out what you should be doing and taking the steps, intimidating as they might seem, to live your dream.

Additionally, Jim has been instrumental in creating loosely organized, but quite effective, networking groups that help connect those seeking to make career changes. These somewhat causal groups are another example of Jim's unique way of doing things. Instead of highly structured workshops where people fill out resume forms and talk about how to use the internet to search for jobs, these groups talk about what people find interesting and what they would like to do. They also share unique ways that participants are combining their desire for fulfillment and the practical need to make a living. People in these groups develop true connections with each other and provide support as they blaze their own trails.

Jim is now comfortable that the work he is doing is what he is meant to do; that work is no longer a separate part of his life, but rather an expression of who he is.

Words of Wisdom from Jim Earley

- What kept me going? Desperation, probably. I had no career left; I had to make this new life work.

- The key is to figure out that making "it" happen is your life's work because when you know what you are meant to do, you don't have any choice. And what you don't know how to do doesn't matter. You will figure it out.

- There are a lot of serendipitous points in my little saga. I just learned to get out of my own way and let it happen.

▲▲▲

Jim Earley, founder of Trailblazer Coaching

CyGen
technologies inc.

JUSTIN GRIEP
Cygentech
www.cygentech.com/

When you meet Justin Griep your first impression is, "This guy is bright." After talking to him for any length of time, you know you are in the presence of a genius. He could lovingly be described as a "techie" but he has that rare ability to explain technology in ways that those of us who never advance beyond "end users" can understand. This combination of technical and communication skills have played a significant role in Justin's success.

Justin developed an interest in computers as a child and had exceptional knowledge and abilities in the computer field by the time he entered high school. While in high school, he participated in the Distributive Education Clubs of America (DECA) program and developed a keen interest in business. DECA's goal is to improve education and career opportunities for students interested in careers in marketing, management, and entrepreneurship. It was through his experience in DECA that he first realized he could, and more importantly, wanted to, pursue business as a career.

> I went to DECA's national conference in Orlando when I was in high school. I was doing the

advertising and visual merchandising category. I remember that we did a role play. I didn't take it all that seriously. Just had fun with it. I got up on stage and won first place in the nation. And that made me think, "Wait a minute. There's some ability I have that I really need to think about."

Justin's first foray into the business world occurred in high school when he was asked to be a computer consultant by a person who owned a computer store. This man wanted to start a software company and was looking for someone to do programming. The man who hired him to do consulting work became his mentor and helped him learn about the business world. Justin could see the advantages of being an independent consultant, and this early work experience fostered his orientation toward working for himself rather than being employed by a company.

From his mentor, Justin learned about the things that aren't in the business books. He developed a keen understanding of what to do and what not to do. The mentor had been a sequential entrepreneur, moving from one opportunity to another. Justin saw this as a pattern he wanted to follow and soon took the leap to start his first business venture.

When Justin finished this initial computer consulting job, he decided to break out on his own as an independent consultant. He'd met some other entrepreneurs in the community. He started working with them designing medical software that proved to be "a lot of fun stuff."

Justin developed an idea for a new business, and he asked a couple of other computer-savvy young men to join him. "Let's turn it from a one-man show to a really powerful team of developers." They agreed. They were eager, but had very limited business experience and had to learn how to do everything—how to get the forms and approvals needed to start the business; how to program their phones; how to run payroll, and, critically important, how to market and get clients. Through hard work, talent, and ingenuity, they developed a successful consulting company called Cygen Technologies. Justin explained the origin of the name.

> Years ago when I was a kid, I saw a word in a dictionary that I just totally loved. It was *Cyclogenisis.* It means the development or creation of a cyclone or hurricane. But people really choked over pronouncing that name, so we shortened it up to Cygen.

Cygen helps organizations who are preparing for a public stock offering assess and manage their systems. Justin's idea was to create a company that would become the product development group for start-up companies and, by doing so, support their growth. In exchange, Cygen would take an equity position in the start-up company. This way, start-up companies, which are frequently short on cash, would have the support they need to meet the demands of becoming a publicly traded entity. At the same time, Justin's equity stake would enable him to be invested in organizations that had the potential for significant growth. Thus, this arrangement could result in mutual gains.

Justin realized the need to focus the services he offered to clients. He didn't have the resources, or the interest to be all things to all people. Consequently, he developed a model that used his organization's knowledge of computers and systems to help improve the performance of other businesses. Justin's computer service company focuses on improving workflow, reducing the amount of paper slowing down the business, and in other ways providing a positive impact on the bottom line.

The exact nature of the work Justin has done has changed over time. When he and his partners started the business, they were helping other start-up companies by becoming their technology developers. They were able to do the development better, cheaper, and faster than most organizations could do it on their own. Justin and his partners assumed an equity position in the companies. Over time they learned that many start-ups fail. When they failed, Cygen's equity interest had little financial value.

They watched different companies make the same business mistakes over and over. Justin wanted to change Cygen's offering so that they could be of more help to their clients, and to improve the long term viability of his organization.

> We chose to move our company over to offering our own software products. After several years of changing the business model and building up our own product line, we are close to launching WorkStreams www.workstreams.com.

> WorkStreams is a combination of productivity Apps that bolt on to Microsoft Office to help businesses run their operations better and improve their performance. WorkStreams is its own brand, wholly owned by CyGen.

Justin knows that the world in which he operates, a combination of business and technology, will continue to change. He intends to modify his work as the needs of the market change and opportunities from new technology emerge. However, regardless of the specific type of products or services he will offer, he anticipates continuing to own a business in the general field of technology and systems.

Words of Wisdom from Justin Griep

- I think it is a bit of the excitement factor that drives entrepreneurs. I want to see things through to the end, but I still anticipate that maybe three years from now, five years from now, I may say, "Okay, I've taken this to a high enough level. I've really achieved as much as I can in this space. Now let me try a different space."

- When I look back, it's interesting how things seem to line up in a way that things happen right when you need them to, or a disaster somehow makes you stronger, or improves a relationship, or teaches you some lessons that you needed to learn.

- To be successful, I think it is extremely important to be able to generate genuine relationships with people.

▲▲▲

CHRISTIANNA HANG
Hmong College Prep Academy
http://hcpak12.org

Like many Hmong immigrants, Christianna Hang and her family endured a perilous journey to the United States. Taking the risk to sail out to sea, hoping for rescue, proved to be a good decision for her family. However, Christianna remembers the sting of being "different" during her grade school years. She recalls the challenges she faced trying to fit in and do well in school while still preserving her culture and retaining her Hmong identity. These childhood experiences, difficult as many of them were, are what gave her the idea to create a school for Hmong students.

> The real idea to create something like Hmong Academy came to me when I needed help as a Hmong student. English is my second language (or my third or fourth language) and I could not get the help I needed. I was in a traditional

school that had a lot of ESL teachers. These people were tremendous helpers to me, but I wanted a learning environment where I could ask questions and not feel stupid, see faces that were the same as my own, and have someone understand what I was going through, and not ask why I didn't eat bread or broccoli. My cultural values and the goals that I had for my education were very important to me. My learning style was totally different from the mainstream and I wanted something that fit me.

Motivated by the desire to improve the educational experience of Hmong youth, Christianna wanted to provide these youngsters with an opportunity that had not been available to her. While in college she observed that an increasing number of Hmong students were getting involved in violent activity and not focusing on their studies.

Back in my country, teachers were like gods. And only the rich and the elite got to go to school. People who were poor like me would have never seen the daylight of education. I saw that many of our children were forgetting the way we grew up and how we looked up to our teachers. So I said, "You know what? There are so many children like myself in the inner city and even suburbs that have no opportunity for a good public education or the likelihood to go to college. If we don't create something to help these kids who are dropping out like flies, what are we going to do? How do we expect any of our Hmong students to go to college? How do we talk about college when students can't even get through middle and high school?"

Seeing this waste of potential contributed to Christianna's motivation to provide an educational experience that supported the students' learning and recognized the value of the Hmong culture. She understood the importance of a rigorous curriculum that would challenge students to think critically and give them confidence that they could face life's challenges. She wanted to instill in students the respect for elders, the sense of responsibility to one's family and the value of being part of a community that she experienced as part of her Hmong heritage. The idea to create such a school stayed dormant in her mind as she completed her own education.

During college she was employed at a charter school where she met an individual who acted as a mentor. That relationship helped Christianna develop her professional skills. Christianna told her mentor about her desire to create a charter school for Hmong students. The mentor provided support and encouragement and helped her learn the process to create a charter school. Christianna sought help from several individuals and government agencies to learn the legal requirements to open and operate a charter school. She found that the bureaucracy associated with such an effort was extensive, entrenched, and slow moving.

She also knew she needed support from Hmong community leaders in order for the school to be successful. She asked friends, who shared her interest in creating such a school, to form a committee to study the feasibility of opening a charter school. Many volunteers were well intentioned, but demands from jobs and families frequently took precedence over working on the feasibility study. Christianna's enthusiasm never diminished. She was the driving force behind the committee and devoted many, many hours to completing the study.

Christianna knew she needed to convince Hmong parents that this school would provide a good opportunity for their children. This was not an easy task. Many Hmong parents were struggling with their own assimilation into American life. They understood about public schools, but the concept of a charter school was confusing and scary. And besides, being in her 30s Christianna was seen as a "kid." Who would trust their children to a kid?

Gradually, the idea of a charter school gained support in the Hmong community, and she was able to involve many individuals in a variety of ways. Once she had support from Hmong community leaders and students' parents, she was able to get the necessary approvals to open a school. Hmong Academy opened in 2004 with about 200 students in grades 9 and 10. In recognition of the school's commitment to preparing students for college, the name was changed to Hmong College Prep Academy. Christianna currently serves as the school's administrator.

Creating the school was a huge undertaking, one that required her dedication and tireless effort. Christianna's determination and extensive hard work brought the idea of this charter school to life. In 2014, the enrollment increased to 1300 students and the school offers classes for kindergarten – 12th grade. In addition to Hmong cultural and linguistic studies, students receive a quality education that prepares them to be successful in college. The school also offers a wide range of extracurricular activities that help the students explore their interests and furthers their sense of being part of a community.

The school has been recognized for its excellence. The 9th – 12th grade high school has achieved "Celebration School Status" which signifies that the high school is among the top

25% of Title I Schools in Minnesota. In comparison to traditional public schools in the Twin Cities, HCPA's graduation rates are 15-20% higher. More than 80% of graduates are attending, or will attend post-secondary education. *US News and World Report* ranks HCPA in the top 39 schools in the state of Minnesota.

Christianna continues to challenge herself and recently completed a doctorate degree in Educational Administration. She has been recognized for her work in education and the community at large. She has been featured in articles in local and national publications and has also served as a speaker for the National Forum on Education Policy, the Minnesota Department of Education NCLB Leadership Institute. She maintains her attitude that, "You don't think about whether or not you can do it, you just do it."

Words of Wisdom from Christianna Hang

- I understand the role of being a strong leader, and I try to be the best servant leader I can. If that means I have to roll up my sleeves and clean up the bathroom, that doesn't bother me.

- I believe that the reason I got this far is that I've believed in the idea and believed I could do it.

- No matter who you are—Hmong, woman, man, whatever—you can make something great happen for the community if you can just put your mind to it and not let people discourage you. Keep going no matter what happens.

▲▲▲

Dr. Christianna Hang, founder and Superintendent for Hmong College Prep Academy, leads the first Hmong-focused high school in the nation, with Hmong literacy and culture integrated into all aspects of learning.

caring BRIDGE.org

SONA MEHRING
CaringBridge
www.caringbridge.org

When Sona Mehring started college, she planned to be a nurse. Her mother was a nurse, and Sona admired how her mother had such a positive effect on people. She saw that compassion and care made a difference, and she wanted to experience that sense of helping other people for herself. However, boredom with her science classes and excitement in her technology class changed her course forever. She discovered the power of technology and wanted to find a way to connect people through technology to better their lives.

Another experience that shaped her future was the opportunity to participate in sports while in college. Sona attended college when women's athletics were gaining in popularity, largely because of the requirements of Title IX. She excelled at sports and sports gave her the opportunity to exercise her leadership skills. Teammates respected her and looked to her for direction. She liked being responsible and saw the possibility that one day she might be a leader.

After graduation, Sona initially pursued a career as a programmer. As her career developed it became clear to her that her life goal was to be the leader of her own business. She wasn't sure about the exact nature of the business she wanted to lead, and she was open to a wide range of possibilities.

"I was always looking for an idea that might go somewhere. You just have to be aware of what is possible."

During her early career, she worked for other organizations and tried a few enterprises of her own. Then in 1997, the needs of some good friends created the circumstances that led to CaringBridge. Her friends had a very premature baby named Brighid and they wanted to keep their family and friends informed as they navigated their way through this health journey. They asked Sona to call people, the standard communication method at the time, to provide them with updates. Sona, who was a web designer, saw this as an opportunity to create a website specifically intended for her friends to share their news and for their family and friends to offer messages of caring and support.

This was during the early days of the internet. The internet was operational, but was still seen as somewhat distant and impersonal. Sona's love for technology, her firm belief that technology could help bring people together, and the specific need of her friends, created the perfect storm that gave birth to CaringBridge. Sona reflected on this initial adventure:

> There was so much being written about technology being cold-hearted and that it was going to rip society apart and it was going to be the end of the world as we knew it. It was wonderful to see an emotional connection bringing compassion alive through technology. I knew the power it could have for people throughout the entire world.

CaringBridge is one of the most widely used healthcare community websites in the world. It allows individuals and families who are experiencing a health crisis, military deployment, or other challenges, to exchange messages with their social network. Giving and getting support during critical times in our lives makes our challenges easier to bear. Sona found her way to merge the power of technology with the need for human love and compassion. From a single need in 1997, Sona has overseen the growth of CaringBridge to its present state, where 46 million visited the site in 2013.

> Brighid's website instantly eased the burden of phone calls and time-consuming, emotional conversations. What I never anticipated—my "wow" moment was the true connection felt by everyone who visited Brighid's website. Those visitors left messages of love and support that were exactly what my friends needed in their incredibly difficult time. The transformation was striking; a simple website became a compassionate community, bringing hope and healing. Brighid's life was a short nine days, but her impact lives on in the hundreds of thousands of CaringBridge sites that have been created since (Mehring, 2010).

At first, Sona worked on CaringBridge as a side business. However it soon became clear that CaringBridge was providing a critical service for many people and that the organization had to grow to respond to this expanding need. CaringBridge users told Sona that many of their families and friends are spread across broad geographic areas. Staying in touch is difficult, particularly during medical or other emergencies. In addition, users expressed appreciation that instead of getting a phone message which once heard is gone, CaringBridge services allowed them to keep messages and read them when they needed encouragement and support the most.

In 2002, Sona made CaringBridge a non-profit organization and devoted herself full-time to building the organization and expanding its services. It was important to her that CaringBridge services are offered free to those who needed them.

Sona initially relied on her friends and colleagues to help the organization develop. As it grew, she also realized the need to bring in experts in critical areas so that CaringBridge could stay current with technological developments and effectively use the emerging social network. In addition, the increasing number of CaringBridge users required that many people be added to the staff to provide the necessary support.

Now with over 70 employees, CaringBridge serves 500,000 people each day and has provided websites for people in all 50 states and in more than 230 countries across the world. CaringBridge has been successful because it provides a highly valued service to a large audience and has the strong support it receives from users and the community. As stated on its website, "Two things make CaringBridge what we are. One is love. The other, donations – our only means of support. We rely on the compassion and generosity of people who believe that no one should ever have to face adversity alone."

CaringBridge remains true to Sona's initial vision. The mission statement, *"To amplify the love, hope and compassion in the world; making each health journey easier"* is more than just a bunch of words to those who work at CaringBridge. The mission is the driving force behind their actions.

Sona has been recognized for her contributions to the field of technology and for her work in the community. She was named one of the Most Influential Women In Technology in 2011 by *Fast Company*, and was a finalist for *Fortune Magazine's* Most Powerful Women Entrepreneurs.

Sona was not part of the original study for my dissertation. I had the opportunity to work with Sona and learned of her journey in creating CaringBridge. I realized she is an excellent example of someone who brought her idea to life. I felt that her story belonged in this book.

Words of Wisdom from Sona Mehring

- Doing something you love—following your passion, you can never really go wrong. (Graham, 2011)

- Out of personal need comes a lot of great ideas. That's what happened to me.

- I was motivated, maybe obsessed, with turning this idea into something anyone, anywhere could use. When I saw the positive impact it had, I knew I had to figure out a way to bring it about.

▲▲▲

Sona Mehring, Founder and CEO of CaringBridge

BERNIE REISBERG
Top Star Group
East Asia Trade

From the time he was a young child, Bernie Reisberg never doubted that someday he would have his own company. He grew up hearing stories about running a business that made it sound exciting and the natural career path for him to follow.

> I grew up in a family with a small business. My father and both of my grandfathers had their own businesses. I thought, if people coming from another country can come to this place and fire up a business in the depths of the Depression, then with a Master's degree in business and international management, a degree in economics, a degree in Chinese language, shame on me if I can't drum something up!

His first opportunity to own a business came earlier than he expected, but when presented with the opportunity, he seized it. While still in college, he and a cousin studied abroad at the University of Shanghai. They had the enthusiasm of youth and the knowledge gained from their studies and family experiences, so starting an Asian art importing business seemed "like the thing to do."

> I started when I was 20 years old with my cousin importing Chinese art. It was the very first thing we did. I know very little about art...But I thought, gee, this looks beautiful to me, so we started importing it.

This business was a short-lived adventure that required frequent international travel. However, Bernie gained valuable experience from this first escapade into the world of global business that prepared him for the creation of his next big idea.

By the time he had completed an MBA, the art importing business had peaked and it was time to move on to something else. He and his business partner knew when they started the art importing company that it would have a limited run so they used it as an opportunity to prepare themselves for greater challenges. Bernie was ready to take on the world and was open to any opportunity that presented itself.

He knew someone in the manufacturing business who provided him with an opportunity to get into the manufacture of sewn goods. He jumped at the chance. Knowing nothing about manufacturing or sewn goods, at the age of 23, he and his business partner cousin launched an international business they called Top Star Group which manufactured gym bags, carry-on luggage and other sewn items. They located their manufacturing facilities in Asia and began searching internationally for buyers for their products. His business partner took a much less active role in developing the company, but was involved financially.

Bernie was clearly aware that he knew little or nothing about manufacturing or running an international business when he started. He knew his lack of knowledge and experience were deficits. He also knew statistics demonstrated the high incidence of failure for new businesses. However, he was confident that he would be successful. This confidence stemmed from an innate belief that hard work and clear thinking, both of which he saw as personal assets, would overcome any obstacles in his way. He didn't see himself as "the brightest guy" but he said, "no one will ever out-work me."

He was cognizant at the outset that there were things he did not know. Throughout the process of creating his idea, he became aware of many more knowledge gaps he had and he experienced some pitfalls that resulted from his lack of experience. He explained that one of the key facts he learned in operating a business is that not all obstacles or challenges are the same.

> I've come to conclude that there are two kinds of obstacles or challenges: The ones you see and the ones you don't see. The ones you see are a piece of cake. It's the ones that you never ever dreamt of that are going to put you out of business.

Over time, Bernie made several changes in his company to respond to changes in the market. He shut down the manufacturing facility in Asia and moved production back to the United States. He added products to his line that would appeal to a wider customer base. Just recently, the focus of the company changed from manufacturing to importing. The name of the company is now East Asia Trade. Coming full circle, he moved production back to East Asia. He imports an even greater range of products: footwear, socks, metal items, and a wide variety of other goods. Bernie recognizes the need to change as conditions change, "You make the best decisions you can, based on the information you have available at the time. But you have to be ready to react as conditions change. You need to be able to deliver what people want when they want it."

He continues to work on developing his ability to see trends, watch for new developments, and operate proactively to stay ahead of the competition. He was driven by the desire to have his own business. Even though he experienced significant obstacles along the way, he never lost faith that he would be successful. This optimism doesn't come from arrogance, but rather from his strong belief that if you work hard and stay open to possibilities, good things will happen. He realizes that in creating and sustaining a new business he has "beaten the odds" and pursues ways to make his business more successful.

Words of wisdom from Bernie Reisberg

- We sort of came into business a bit backwards in that we really didn't have any wild dreams or newfangled inventions or ideas. We just thought this is something that we ought to be able to do. So we did. I guess what kept us in the business was this optimism.

- I know that I may make a mistake, but then it will be my mistake. And I'm going to live with that mistake and go forward. You can't be overwhelmed by your mistakes.

- I think that in my case I looked at business as this is what I'm supposed to do. This is what I wanted to do. I never thought I would do anything else.

▲▲▲

SISTER JEAN THUERAUF
Cookie Cart
www.cookiecart.org

Sister Jean Thuerauf, a Catholic nun, brought many ideas to fruition. She dedicated her life to helping residents of the Near North Side, an economically depressed, high crime area of Minneapolis. Sister Jean's idea explored in this study was the creation of a bakery, the Cookie Cart. It is much more than just a bakery. It employs at-risk youth, provides them with education and valuable work experiences, and engages adult volunteers to work with these young people. Sister Jean sees herself as an instrument who helps fulfill ideas inspired by God, rather than being the originator of her ideas. She believes she is listening to God and doing what God directs her to do.

Earlier in her ministry, Sister Jean moved from the comfort of suburbia to the troubled neighborhood she sought to serve. When she arrived, she had no idea what her ministry would look like. She set about learning the real needs of the community and how she might serve them.

> I had no idea, no idea about a Cookie Cart when I came here. It evolved out of a circumstance. I had to find out what the real life was. So I went around establishing relationships to find out who these people really are and what they needed. . . I found the children had no structure to their lives. I watched and listened, and I lived with them.

Many young children came to her home after school. Her home provided a nurturing environment for these children, most of whom had little stability in their own homes. She welcomed the children, helped with their homework, read Bible stories to them, and provided supervised activities. She offered a safe haven and gave children an alternative to the gangs, drugs, and violence that were so prevalent in the neighborhood.

As the children grew, she looked for activities that provided them a sense of accomplishment. She found that baking cookies was a particularly worthwhile and enjoyable experience for the children. Following a recipe, mixing the ingredients, and happily eating the results of their efforts demonstrated the value of doing a job well. Many of these children lived in very challenging environments and received little encouragement or positive reinforcement.

She started baking cookies with them on a regular basis. The more often they baked, the more obvious it became that baking was a simple way for them to get a sense of accomplishing something positive. Sister Jean said, "I wanted them to see that they could do something worthwhile. I wanted them to get a picture of the great person they could be."

Fresh-baked goodies are always a welcome treat for children, but they were prolific bakers. Even their eager appetites could only consume a limited number of these tasty baked goods. Sister Jean began looking for ways to use the cookies to generate income to help support her ministry with the children. Some of the first customers of the Cookie Cart were churches who bought the goodies to serve after Mass on Sunday. Soon the cookie business expanded beyond what her kitchen could handle. Sister Jean started looking for a bakery.

She engaged many people in creating the bakery. She had previously served a parish in a wealthy suburb of Minneapolis. She contacted individuals from that parish to not only buy cookies, but also to find volunteers who would help her launch the bakery as a business. In addition, she approached many residents and business owners in the Near North Side and asked for their help. She called on others from her extensive network of contacts throughout the city. With help from local businesses, Sister Jean was able to buy a building, convert it into a bakery and operate it as a business. She related this story about how she secured the site for Cookie Cart.

> I drove down Emerson, and there is this building. . . .the glass is broken, there is no electricity, and no one had been in it for years. I called this fellow who owned the building and said I wanted to see him and he said, "Come over." He knew I wanted something, so he said, "What do you want?" And I said, "Well, I want that old building." He said, "You don't want that old building,

you don't know what it is really like," and I said, "You don't know how I'm going to fix it up. I have 19 people ready to help me." And he said, "Oh my," and we agreed and transacted our little thing, and I got hold of the 19 people and told them to bring their flash lights. And they came and they saw the potential in there.

And so they began. They worked hard. The building needed extensive repairs and there were numerous licenses and approvals that needed to be secured. Sister Jean also had to acquire baking equipment. She admitted she really didn't know what she needed. Sister Jean approached the owner of a large local bakery and asked if he had any old equipment they no longer needed that might help her get started. He told her, "We are going to close a bakery and I can give you some equipment." The next day he brought in an industrial mixer and other equipment worth over $10,000, giving her nearly everything she needed to open the bakery. Sister Jean saw this as another example that God was making this all happen. "You see, the Lord listened to our needs and we got what we needed."

With Sister Jean leading the charge, and so many others joining the fight, the bakery became a reality. Adults supervised and ran the business and the young people made the cookies. Their success continued, and in 1996, the bakery moved to a larger facility where the students are now participating in the business operations.

The bakery contracted with service organizations to involve developmentally disabled youth in the baking process and these teens also benefit from the positive, supportive environment evident at the Cookie Cart. The Cookie Cart has always been about more than just making great cookies, although I can attest that the cookies are delicious! Baking and performing other tasks provide teens with meaningful work. It helps them learn life and leadership skills through work experience and training.

In addition to on the job training, the Cookie Cart offers its employees classroom instruction on customer service and financial literacy. Student workers also have the opportunity to achieve the National Career Readiness Certification (NCRC). This certification requires diligent study to achieve and when awarded, demonstrates to prospective employers that a teen has the foundational skills necessary to be successful in the workplace.

Sister Jean believed that her success was possible because of inspiration and intervention from God. Creating the bakery was part of her much larger vision of living a life of service, directed by God's hand.

Words of Wisdom from Sister Jean Thuerauf

- Building the Cookie Cart was a way to do God's work. It seems that at every step, the Lord was right there with the answer for us. He was ahead of us.

- It is more than just me. It is all the people coming together with the same goal. So many people got involved, no way could we fail.

- What you give, you get back.

▲▲▲

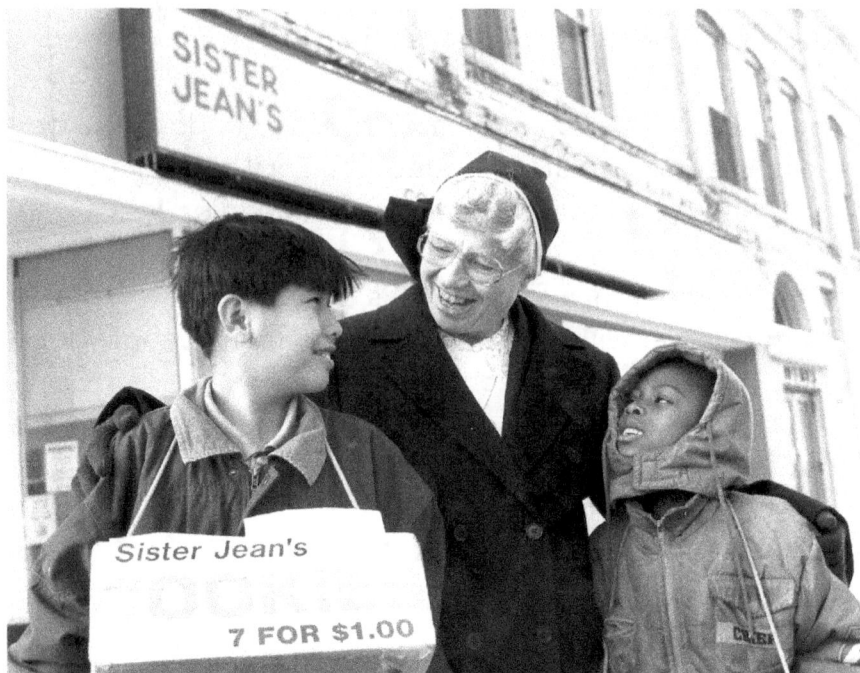

Sister Jean Thuerauf in the early days of the Cookie Cart.

The previous stories were examples of individuals working primarily alone to bring their ideas to life. As we will discuss later, no one in this study worked completely alone. Everyone needed to involve other individuals to some degree at various stages in the development of the entity they created. However these first stories were about individuals who conceived their ideas by themselves.

In some cases, the idea for creating something new was shared by a spouse, partner, or colleague, and working together, two people jointly created the entity. The following stories are about pairs of people who intentionally worked together to create their shared vision.

CHARLIE AND MARIA GIRSCH
Creativity Central

Charlie and Maria Girsch are a married couple who developed Creativity Central, a training and consulting business. It is fitting that Charlie and Maria created a company that is about helping people explore alternatives and find new ways of doing things because their very lives have been about change and creating something new.

Charlie's path to Creativity Central meandered in many different directions. He spent several years as a priest on Chicago's South Side. He then moved to the Twin Cities and developed a job training program for a large employer. Changing his career focus yet again, Charlie helped set up St. Paul's Model Cities program. Later, he served as Deputy Director of the St. Paul Urban Coalition. After all these experiences, Charlie made the leap into the creativity arena and took a job as a toy and game designer.

Maria also had a rather circuitous route to toy designing. She was once a nun. She became a certified French teacher and developed "French by the Fireside," an innovative program for adults wanting to learn French. She has a Master's degree in Human Development, with a concentration in creativity and life-long learning, two of her strongest interests. Together, Charlie and Maria were successful toy inventors for over 25 years. They licensed over 200 products worldwide and hold several US and International patents.

In the '90s, the toy industry was undergoing changes that made it harder for the individual inventor to prosper. Large corporations were dominating the field and the use of electronics in toys made it nearly impossible for independent inventors to compete. Charlie and Maria were aware that they would have to venture into another industry in order to continue making a living using their innovation skills. They applied their own creative talents and the practice they developed to create toys, asking themselves, "What if. . ." and "What's next?" to help them find new ways to stay connected with creativity.

Charlie and Maria knew that although they shared common values, they had complementary, but very different creative talents. Maria could generate a plethora of new ideas and Charlie was able to refine the ideas into practical applications. In addition, Charlie noted,

> Her fears are complimented by my riskiness.
> My stream of consciousness is balanced by her
> organizational writing skills. She is the hunter. I
> am the gatherer. But we both seem to thrive on
> stimulation. We need it, want it, look for it. So
> there is a wonderful convergence that happens
> when we work together.

They combined their varied talents as they pursued finding a new way to use creativity as the basis for their work. They read books, talked to other people and then learned of a certificate program on innovative creative thinking that seemed to be just what they were looking for to help them take the next step.

Charlie attended this 13 week program and when he came home after each session, he shared what he learned with Maria. More than just picking up terminology and techniques, Maria also caught Charlie's enthusiasm for what he was learning. The class helped him think about ways of applying their creativity to something other than inventing. He and Maria realized that their ability to invent was something that could be transferred outside of the toy industry. They thought they could help people understand the process they used to create their inventions. Although they were unsure exactly how they would do it, the idea of teaching people about creativity was appealing. It meant they could take care of practical things, like earning a living, and also feed their desire to be innovative.

Maria and Charlie were confident that everyone has creative skills inside them, but sometimes, these skills were "resting." They wanted to help people wake them up and experience the fun of being creative. Inventing toys wasn't the only way to have fun.

Their initial forays into the training and consulting world were sessions with friends or acquaintances in which Charlie and Maria presented what they had learned about the creative process. They developed individual and group activities to help those attending the workshop realize and access their own creativity. Additionally, they had the opportunity to work with school children and a church group. After doing so, they were even more convinced they had something to share that would help others experience their own creativity.

Charlie and Maria wrote a book that outlined some of what they had learned about creativity. The couple worked together along with one of their children, who was a commercial artist, to create this unique book. The book, *Fanning the Creative Spirit*, was designed not only to provide information about creativity, but also the very nature of the book demonstrated what a creative approach looks like. The book was printed in a non-standard size, used different fonts and formatting throughout the book, and included several different colored pages and drawings that add interest and energy. The end result was a unique paperback that had a different look than that of a "traditional" book—the exact image they sought to create.

As word spread about their unique approach to creativity, they started getting calls from individuals and organizations looking for programs on creativity. In response to these requests, Charlie and Maria established their own training and consulting business which they named Creativity Central. They consulted with individuals and groups who were interested in increasing their ability to think in new ways and introduced them to the "Girsch" creative problem solving process they'd developed.

They continue to share the message that everyone is creative and can learn to access their inherent creative talents. They present programs on idea generation for sales and marketing groups and others looking for new ways to think about their products and services. They have helped groups that are stuck at a certain point in a process and need an extra push to reinvigorate their creative energies. They are also are featured speakers at national and international conferences and retreats.

Charlie and Maria continue to exercise their creativity as they pursue other interests beyond Creativity Central. Their current adventure is pursuing a family connectivity technology. Although in their 70s, they are drawn to bringing new ideas to life.

Words of Wisdom from Charlie and Maria Girsch

- I just believed that we could do it and we did, but not the way I imagined.

- The two of us look at each other and wonder how we did this. This is so fun. Fun is important.

- The jump from toys was a big one, and that is probably where I had my biggest doubt, but that didn't last more than five minutes. I think we worked hard at it, but I think we have the right instincts for it.

▲▲▲

Charlie and Maria Girsch, founders of Creativity Central.

BILL AND NANCY LASCHEID
Neighborhood Health Clinic
www.neighborhoodhealthclinic.org

Bill and Nancy Lascheid are a married couple who created a medical clinic that serves the working poor in Collier County, Florida. Both are healthcare professionals with many years of experience in a variety of medical practices. Bill is a doctor and Nancy is a nurse. During their earlier careers they provided health care to the poor and found this work rewarding. When they retired, they knew that they wanted to do something constructive and continue their life's mission to help the poor. They recognized the critical role adequate health care plays in the life of individuals and the community. They were aware of the challenges faced by the working poor—those individuals who are not provided medical coverage from their place of employment and also do not qualify for government provided medical assistance.

On one of their first days as official "retirees," they discussed their desire to do something meaningful with their lives. They knew they had the medical knowledge and experience to provide health care to those who could not afford traditional medical services. And, they knew they could volunteer at a free clinic—but they wanted to do more.

In one marathon discussion session of twenty-three hours, they developed an outline of a business plan and a vision and mission statement which described what they wanted to create.

> We knew the demographics. We knew the challenges. We knew what we had to have. And when we were finished, at the end of the day and a night and a day, we had a plan. We had a one page plan. We didn't use one preposition. We made everything nouns and verbs. It was very simple.

Their goal was to open a clinic where the working poor could receive high quality medical care, provided in an atmosphere of respect and dignity. As part of maintaining the patient's dignity, they realized the importance of finding a way that patients could have some partnership in their health care (i.e. pay what was affordable for them).

They knew what they wanted for the end result and then had to determine how to move from their one page plan to an actual clinic. Nancy and Bill couldn't undertake such an endeavor alone and identified individuals who worked in the professions they would need, such as doctors, nurses, pharmacists, accountants, and other business associates. They contacted people they knew in each profession and asked them to participate in a meeting during which they presented their idea to create a new kind of clinic.

At the end of the one hour meeting, everyone was convinced that the plan could work and expressed their willingness to help create the clinic. Over the next two weeks, each person worked in their own area to bring together the necessary resources to make the clinic a reality. At their second meeting, they had all the elements they needed to create the clinic. However, they also identified a major obstacle: they had to find a way for medical professionals to be covered by malpractice insurance when they volunteered at the clinic. Undaunted by what most people might see as an insurmountable barrier, Nancy took on the challenge and, with the help of others, was able to get special legislation enacted by the state of Florida that resolved the issue. As described by one of her associates, "Nancy might be a tiny person, but she is a huge presence. People listen to her."

The couple worked tirelessly, maneuvering through the political, legal and business challenges they faced. They generated a lot of excitement about forming the clinic and felt they had to "seize the moment" and move quickly.

> We did an unthinkable thing. We set an opening date of three months. The reason for this is that we knew that if we didn't make a commitment that was unrealistic, we weren't going to do it. So we said three months. Everyone told us we were crazy, and yet we opened in three months.

The clinic was an overwhelming success. After one year, they expanded to a new, much larger facility that enabled them to expand their services, including same day surgical procedures. One of the features of the clinic that contributes to its success is the inclusion of an onsite pharmacy. Having the pharmacy right down the hall removes barriers for patients who may have difficulty securing transportation to get to a different location to pick up their medications.

They were able to move to the bigger, better equipped facility, largely from the very generous donations of two unaffiliated individuals. Both inquired about the clinic and Nancy sent them reports. Each said that earlier in their lives they would have qualified to be patients at the clinic, and now that they had achieved a level of financial success, they wanted to support the work being done at the clinic. The Lascheids were blown away. They hadn't anticipated being able to provide more extensive services at such an outstanding facility. These incidents, and others, convinced them that creating the clinic was their destiny, controlled by a higher power.

The clinic addresses a significant need in the local community. It has broad based support from foundations, businesses, service clubs, civic organizations and communities of faith, and does not accept government funding. There are over 700 people who donate their time to the Neighborhood Clinic, including 247 physicians and 119 nurses (Stanley, C. 2013).

The Lascheids are recognized for their community service and have received numerous awards, including the Point of Light Award from the state of Florida, the National Jefferson Award for Public Service, the Partners in Medicine Award from the Florida Medical Association, and the Humanitarians of the Year for 2012 from Hodges University.

Over the last few years, Nancy and Bill have reduced their role in the day-to-day leadership of the clinic. Their daughter, Leslie, was selected by a search committee to take on the role of CEO. Like her parents, Leslie is committed to getting things done, caring for people, and providing the best possible treatment for the patients of the Neighborhood Clinic.

Recently, the clinic added multiple patient education programs and participated in two medical research studies. The clinic has been studied by others across the country and is considered a model for those looking for a solution to providing quality medical care for the working poor. When I visited the facility, I was impressed by the warm, welcoming atmosphere. Patients were given excellent, attentive treatment from caring professionals. Patients were listened to and treated with dig-nity. Truly this is a model for *all* medical clinics.

Words of Wisdom from Nancy and Bill Lascheid

- So many things just happened. When we needed money desperately; when we needed a certain kind of doctor; when we needed good publicity; anytime we needed something, it just plain happened. That is divine intervention. A higher power was driving the bus.

- The idea was so simplistic that everyone could em-brace it. It took on a life of its own.

- I never doubted that we would get what we needed, and I think the reason is because of the quality of the people who came and joined us in bringing this con-cept to life.

▲▲▲

Dr. Bill and Nancy Lascheid receive the Humanitarians of the Year
award.
Photo by Naples (Fla.) Daily News

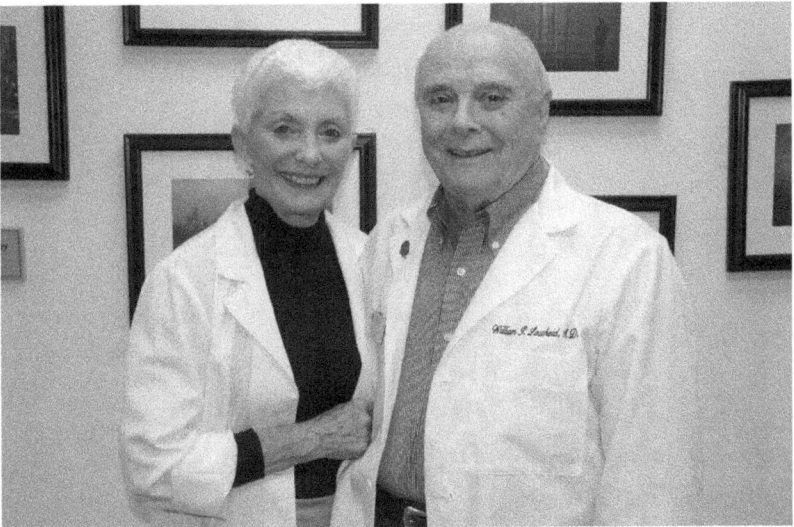

Nancy and Bill Lascheid, founders of the Neighborhood Clinic

The current Neighborhood Clinic

The original, three room Neighborhood clinic.

water for people
everyone | forever

KEN MILLER AND JACK MANNION
Water For People
https://www.waterforpeople.org

Ken Miller and Jack Mannion were instrumental in creating Water For People, an international organization that helps impoverished people worldwide improve their quality of life by supporting sustainable drinking water, sanitation, and hygiene. Ken Miller had worked in the water utility field for several years when he developed the idea to create such an organization. He learned thousands of children died every day because of water-borne diseases that are preventable. The following statistics kept resurfacing in his mind:

> The World Health Organization announced that 6,000 – 8,000 children died every day of water-borne diseases that we could have stamped out 100 years ago with simple chlorination. So there was a real guilt among professionals in the water supply business. The idea of 8,000 children dying per day was a real throat clincher for me.

Ken felt compelled to do something to address this tragic loss of life. The United Nations, World Bank, and other international organizations were aware of the problem and saw it as a high priority, but no one was offering an effective solution. Some organizations had made furtive attempts at providing safe water to impoverished communities, but few had any sustainable success.

Not long after Ken learned of the number of deaths of children due to unsafe water, he was elected president of the American Water Works Association (AWWA). One of his goals was to do something to address the water situation in communities in third-world countries. He suggested that AWWA reach out to these communities and partner with them to address their problems. He began by involving others in the water utility industry, and brought Jack Mannion into the organization.

Jack had extensive experience in management and had helped other organizations realize their goals. He brought his experience and confidence to the project. Bringing drinkable water to communities throughout the third world was a daunting task, particularly since others had tried and were not successful. However, his previous success solving other difficult problems helped build his confidence that he was able to tackle this challenge. He understood the difference between confidence and arrogance. He wanted to avoid the hubris of the ignorant who expected a simple solution to solve a complex problem. He knew his limits, but welcomed the challenge.

> I would never take on something so far beyond me that I knew I couldn't do it. That would be stupid of me. And there are some things that even now I can say that's not for me; it's over my head. But to go one step or two steps beyond where you are is, I think, reachable—it's doable.

Together, and with the involvement of many others, Ken and Jack created a unique and effective solution to improving the water quality of poor communities in various locations throughout the world. One of their keys to success was the amount of person to person interaction they had within the communities they wanted to serve. Unlike some other organizations, Water For People didn't just send supplies and manuals to these areas, but rather many individuals traveled internationally to visit these communities that didn't have adequate clean water.

On these visits, they sought to identify ways of correcting the problem and collaborated with the local citizens and authorities. They spent a lot of time asking questions and learning the culture of the area. A key to their success was that they respected the opinions of the people as to which options would work in their communities. They didn't come into the community as the "experts" who were going to tell these people what to do. Rather, they helped educate the people to help them make the best decisions for their communities. The local people made the decisions and took responsibility for the on-going success of the project.

Ken and Jack soon realized that providing clean water was only part of the solution. Many other programs that installed water systems had been unsuccessful in the long term because the people using these systems were unable to maintain the equipment and didn't understand the basics of sanitation. To be sustainable, the local community had to assume responsibility for maintaining the clean water system. To do so they needed education, training, and support.

Ken established Water For People as a not-for-profit association and invited colleagues to join him in this effort to bring sustainable clean water systems to impoverished areas throughout the world. Once the association was established, they involved professional organizations, consultants, manufacturers, academics, people working in regulatory agencies and other utilities, and began projects in several areas that suffered from a shortage of potable water. They refined their processes on each new project and now have a well-defined system that has demonstrated significant success. By 2007, they had more than 400 sustainable projects in operation.

An example of the type of projects supported by Water For People comes from Guatemala. In the rainy season, water is plentiful, but from November to April there is little or no rain. Prior to involvement with Water For People, mothers carried water to school every day for their children to drink, make snacks, and to wash dishes. The water often came from unsafe sources and, as a result, the children became sick. A group of mothers worked with Water For People who helped create a plan for a 50,000 liter rain catchment tank and created hand washing stations for the children. Local officials were involved in the project. The result is that the community has become more aware of how to take advantage of the water when it is plentiful during the rainy season, and how to ration it effectively during dry spells.

Another example comes from a community in Honduras whose water system failed, and the community had to return to their old, unsanitary system. The local water board worked with Water For People and the city to rehabilitate their water system. They also installed water micrometers, which help residents be conscious of their water usage. They are learning how to protect the water resource for their future use. Water For People provided information and support to the water board, and it is now a strong and sophisticated group. The water board created a monthly water tariff that equals about $2.60 USD so that the community will have enough money for maintenance of the current system and will be prepared for the eventual replacement of their water system.

Ken and Jack's personal and professional history demonstrated their honesty and integrity and was a key to gaining support from their community and water quality organizations. They had a solid reputation as trustworthy and honorable individuals. Those who supported their efforts were confident that their investment of time, effort, and financial resources would be used properly to achieve the desired result.

The organization Ken and Jack helped form continues to attract employees who are dedicated to the cause. One employee I met on a visit to the Water For People office told me that there are many days when she is wrapping up her work for the day and she remembers the 6,000 – 8,000 children who will die each day from water-borne illnesses. This knowledge frequently causes her to work just a little longer to try to put a dent in that most disturbing number. Ken and Jack's passion lives on.

Water For People is recognized for its effectiveness. It was designated by AWWA as the charity of choice, and is also endorsed by several other organizations, such as the Water Environment Federation, the Water Quality Association, the National Association of Water Companies, the National Association of Clean Water Agencies, and the Association of Metropolitan Water Agencies.

Words of Wisdom from Jack Mannion and Ken Miller

- I think anybody starting a new venture needs to think about: Why are we doing this? What are we trying to do and who are we trying to do it for? And if you don't have a niche that is not met by anybody else, you better not go into it.

- I loved the challenge of creating something out of nothing that was responding to a need. I got a kick out of seeing the reaction of the public saying, "Yes! This is wonderful! I want to be a part of that and I'll join and put my money where my mouth is."

- It's been a labor of love. I've had a good time doing it. Seeing it grow is great. The quality of people, the devotion and time that they put into it—it's fantastic.

▲▲▲

Water For People's "Everyone Forever" program seeks to ensure that throughout the world, everyone will have a sustainable source of clean water.

"We want water for everyone, forever."

DICK AND FLORENCE NOGAJ
Harvest for Humanity
and Jubilation Housing

Dick and Florence Nogaj created an agricultural business that paid all workers a livable wage. They also developed a companion housing community that provides farm workers the opportunity for affordable housing and home ownership. The idea for these specific initiatives came during a vacation at a beautiful and luxurious resort not far from the future location of the farm and housing community. While surrounded by luxury and comfort, Dick and Florence learned of a strike by farm workers in a neighboring community, Immokalee, Florida. They investigated the situation and learned that right in the middle of one of the richest areas in the country, the living conditions of farm workers were on a par with those of the third world. They decided to do something to address this situation.

> We vacationed on Sanibel Bell Island and
> we read about a hunger strike going on in
> Immokalee. We decided we are at a point that
> we know we are not going to spend the rest
> of our lives on a golf course in Naples. So we
> drove to Immokalee and we discovered, much
> to our distress, third world poverty here, in the
> United States, in the richest county in the coun-
> try. It was just astounding. So it led us to in-
> vestigate the systemic causes that we had such
> poverty here (D. Nogaj).

Dick had been a successful businessman. When he decided to retire from running his engineering firm, he sold his
company to his employees. He and his wife lived comfortably,
but not lavishly. Therefore they had the financial resources to
invest in a new endeavor. They were eager to create an entity
aligned with their personal values.

In their past, they had been involved in many charitable
and community activities. Florence had served as the chair
of the board for an alternative school in Chicago and helped
save it from going under, which was quite an accomplishment.
Florence and Dick had been instrumental in creating a Habitat
for Humanity program outside of Chicago and saw the positive
impact such investments have on a community. Over a two-
year period, their involvement with Habitat for Humanity took
them to a variety of locations, including the Dominican Republic,
where they experienced third-world living conditions. They saw
the devastation of poverty and the significant changes that a little help could bring. They were prepared to take on a new challenge that would draw on their business skills and experience.

In addition to adequate financial resources, Dick and Florence
possessed the passion and commitment needed to see their

idea through to completion. Their personal values called for them to make a contribution to those in need. Dick said he felt a sense that we are all obligated to use our talents for the betterment of our communities. He believed that people should share what they have with those less fortunate, whether it is talent, time, or financial resources. Florence and Dick saw the creation of a farm that paid fair wages and a housing project that met the needs of the workers as a spiritual journey.

> I think for us this journey is one of recognizing and being consciously aware of people that come into our lives that are not accidental. There is a reason for the interrelationships that occur and I think that reason is to make this place a better world somehow, some way. We have to keep concentrating on the commitment to leave the world a better place than we found it. One thing we can all agree on, none of us is taking it with us (D. Nogaj).

When they were first exposed to the poverty and poor living conditions of the farm workers, they knew nothing about farming. Their overwhelming sense that they were supposed to do something to address the needs they saw outweighed their concerns about a lack of knowledge and experience in the field. Dick said, "You can always find the information you need, but without the commitment, you go nowhere." Dick contacted experts in the field and soon saw the relationship between food prices and farm wages and the resulting, revolving pattern of poverty for farm workers. He decided to develop a business venture that would provide living wages and desirable housing for the farm workers, thus laying the foundation for a vibrant community.

We wanted to develop a new alternative farming model that would pay living wages. It would not just demonstrate an idea or concept. Ideas are a dime a dozen. Only if you can turn them into reality and enjoy the benefits of the project are you really going to make a difference and bring about a paradigm shift, which is what we think agriculture badly needed. When it comes to farm workers, the system is badly broken and needs to be fixed. We felt we could start the beginning of the end of poverty with the new farming model that would pay living wages and eventual ownership.

Dick realized he needed help in making the model work. Therefore, he collaborated with a university to identify a product that could grow in that geographical area. He also learned the farming techniques required to raise and harvest the produce. He discovered that blueberries were an upscale product that could flourish in the area and could also command a premium price in the market. A few cents more per pound was enough to provide the level of income needed to make the fair wage farm function. Dick acquired land to begin the farm he named Harvest for Humanity. The farm pays workers, both those on permanent staff and seasonal workers, a fair, livable wage.

The affordable housing project, called Jubilation, was developed in conjunction with Harvest for Humanity. Jubilation is a planned community offering amenities such as a park, soccer field, basketball court, walking paths and a community center. The overall impression of the Jubilation Housing Community is pleasant and prosperous; not a typical cookie cutter, government–subsidized housing project. A great deal of attention was paid to the architecture and landscaping so that the development is appealing and feels like a "community."

Florence took on the challenge of helping the potential residents of Jubilation secure loans to purchase homes. Many of these individuals would not qualify for conventional mortgages. She used her network of community leaders, her powers of persuasion, and ample patience to work with local financial institutions to get residents financial assistance, thus allowing many to purchase homes for the first time. Their goal was to provide an ownership option for those who work on the farm and others who live in the community.

Harvest for Humanity and Jubilation have been studied by community activists throughout the country. It is considered a new model that could positively affect other economically depressed farming communities.

Unfortunately, the blueberry farm was destroyed by a hurricane in 2005, and despite their efforts, the Nogajs were not able to recreate a viable farm operation under their ownership. However, they initially leased, then sold the land to a farmer who employs farm workers and pays them fair wages. The Jubilation Housing project has survived and still provides affordable housing for farm workers and others of limited means. It, like all other real estate, rode the roller-coaster created by the recent recession. The good news is that the community is still the pleasant, inviting neighborhood it was created to be. The destruction of the farm and the financial challenges of the housing community, although not welcomed, didn't dampen the Nogaj's commitment to make the best of the situation and keep their vision of helping those in poverty alive and well.

Dick wrote a book, *Don't Retire, Get Inspired: One Couple's Extraordinary Journey to Make a Difference* that relates his and Florence's experiences with Habitat for Humanity, Harvest for Humanity and Jubilation and other charitable activities. Recently, they purchased an office building outside of Chicago that provides operating space for non-profit organizations at 25% of the regular rental rates. These organizations cover a wide range of services and serve many different communities. Having such significantly reduced rent allows many worthwhile organizations to thrive and use their funds for their charitable purposes instead of rent.

Dick and Florence continue to find ways to make a meaningful difference and to leave their part of the world, a better place.

> There is a finite amount of resources in the world and they are there so that everyone can live in prosperity. I don't need to live in the fanciest house. I think we are all here for a purpose: a purpose greater than just making money and having the most toys.

Words of Wisdom from Dick and Florence Nogaj

- Many people said, "That's a nice idea, but it will never happen." The more they told us it was impossible, the more committed we were to making it happen. Be tenacious and persuasive and never take "no" for an answer.

- We had a lot of timely coincidences that we call miracles as we traveled down the road on this journey.

- I don't hang onto things. I build them, give them wings and make sure they are as sustainable as I can make them.

▲▲▲

Jubilation Housing Community

3

Common Themes

▲

Whereas each situation described in this book was different and each person's experience reflected this difference, the commonalities that emerged from an analysis of the data were pronounced. The patterns that existed across all the participants became easily identifiable after a thorough analysis of all the data I collected. I carefully coded the responses I received from each person I interviewed and compared the results systematically so that I was certain that the themes I identified were common to all participants. I had colleagues review my work to ensure that I was interpreting the data correctly. I also asked the participants to review my conclusions. My colleagues and the participants agreed with my conclusions.

Some factors were shared by some of the participants in this study, but were not common to all. For example, some of the participants felt that they were moved to accomplish the creation of their idea by a higher power, but others didn't have this experience. Another example of a factor shared by some and not all was that some participants had readily available financial resources that helped them create their entity; whereas others had to scramble to find funding they needed to bring their idea to life.

The five common themes described in the next chapters are the result of analyzing extensive information gathered for this study and identifying commonalities. Only factors that were common for all participants are represented as a theme. The themes help explain why the participants pursued the specific idea, the processes used by the participants to further the development of their idea, and characteristics common to all participants. The themes that emerged from the research are:

1. **Vision**: Implementing this specific idea was realization of the future the participants desired for their lives.

▲

2. **Engaging Others**: Getting cooperation and support from other people whose participation was necessary for the idea to become real.

▲

3. **Flexible Processes and Plans**: Processes and plans had to change as circumstances required.

▲

4. **Commitment**: A combination of tenacity and resourcefulness that drove the participants to completion.

▲

5. **Positive Attitude**: An overall positive attitude about life.

You are not here merely to make a living. You are here in order to enable the world to live more amply, with greater vision, with a finer spirit of hope and achievement. You are here to enrich the world, and you impoverish yourself if you forget the errand.

Woodrow Wilson

4

Vision

▲

The participants in this study were motivated to pursue their idea because the idea was a means by which they could achieve their purpose—what they saw as a life goal. The presence of a clearly defined purpose and desired future state fostered their acceptance of the idea as a vehicle to achieve their vision. As used in this study, *vision* refers to having a distinct, desired future outcome in mind. Sometimes the way to achieve the vision was not initially evident to participants, but everyone had a clearly defined purpose and could articulate their desired future state.

The vision didn't always manifest itself as a picture of exactly what they would create; instead, having the vision drove them to create the entity that served their purpose. For example, Stan Appelbaum said, "I didn't really have a big vision; I just wanted to help a couple of hundred kids." Helping the kids was his vision. Friends of Foster Children was the way he achieved his vision.

Nancy Lascheid knew what she wanted to achieve long before she found a way to do it. The vision she and her husband shared was clear and guided their actions and their decision to create a clinic that manifested their desire to serve the needs of the poor.

It wasn't an idea for a clinic; it was recognition of a need. . . My husband and I made a very conscious decision to do two things. Number one was to seek out community service projects that dealt with the underbelly of life—the negatives of our society. And the second thing was to volunteer to participate at whatever level they needed our skills.

Christianna Hang was an exemplar of clear purpose and vision. From an early age, she knew she wanted to create a school dedicated to educational excellence and helping children achieve. The mission of the school she created reflects her vision: "*Hmong College Prep Academy's mission is to provide the best integrated, challenging, and well-rounded educational experience to students in grades K-12.*"

Sona Mehring spoke of her creation of CaringBridge not as just a dream, but her destiny. She felt this was the path she was meant to take. She was driven by three separate desires. The first was to have a positive impact on people's lives. The second was to use the power of technology to create community. And third, she wanted to own her own business. CaringBridge was the vortex where these three elements fused.

Dick Nogaj was also certain about his vision. He saw an unmet need in the farming community that he felt he could address. His goal was to help the poor and make the world a better place. The way to do so was a farm that paid workers fair wages and Jubilation, which provided the opportunity for affordable housing.

Ken Miller had a clear vision to reduce water-borne illnesses and lessen human suffering related to a lack of potable water. He visualized the desired future of creating sustainable water and sanitation systems in communities in all parts of the world.

Sister Jean Thuerauf was driven by a deep sense of purpose based on her definition of herself as an instrument of the Lord. She believed God placed her in the challenging environment in which she lived to serve the people there. She reflected, "My life's work is to bring community to this community." However, she initially had no idea she would fulfill her life's mission of serving the Lord and the community by creating a bakery. The bakery was an instrument to achieve her vision of creating a healthy, safe community. Helping to establish such a community served her vision, which was to serve the Lord.

Sister Jean understood the value of having a positive vision, particularly for children who regularly encountered threats to their safety and well-being. Her vision of a healthy community included having children who lived in that area develop their own positive visions for their futures. She understood that many of the children didn't believe that they had options. She wanted them to have hope and a sense that they could achieve their goals. "The important thing is that they realize their lives have many possibilities and it's up to them to make responsible choices" (Sister Jean Thuerauf as cited in Norwood, 1996). Her vision of "making their troubled lives more humane" was always evident to her. "The Holy Spirit has sent me here to help build God's kingdom on earth. That's the mission" (Sister Jean Thuerauf as cited in Ball, 2002).

Jim Earley had a specific goal in mind. He knew what he wanted, but never in his wildest dreams did he think he would get what he wanted by starting his own business. Instead, he defined his desired future as "merging his way of making an income with his life's work." How he would accomplish his vision became evident as the phenomenon of moving from concept to implementation unfolded. He came to realize that the vehicle to bring his vision to life was to do something he feared, start his own business.

Others had a vision of realizing their own financial and personal development goals by creating an entity that met a need for those who would buy their products or services. Bernie Reisberg, Justin Griep, Sona Mehring, and Charlie and Maria Girsch all had clear visions of creating their own businesses— their desired future. The exact nature of the business was not initially obvious, but the desire to own their own business was a distinct and purposeful vision.

These participants had a sense that managing their own company was the only way they were going to earn a living. None of them seriously considered the option of working for someone else as a long-term career choice. Their desired future was clear and distinct.

Charlie and Maria Girsch also saw creating their new business as a way to stay connected to something they loved— creativity—and to replace what had been their previous jobs. They recognized that there were people who were looking for ways to expand their creativity. Charlie and Maria could meet this need and not only continue to develop their own creative talents, but also provide themselves financial rewards.

Although there was no consistent pattern as to the onset of the idea, the idea represented a way to bring a vision to life for all of the participants. The idea gave shape and substance to their vision. The concept was initially developed and accepted by the participants because it enabled a desired future state they wanted to create. The clear vision was why, of all the thoughts that entered their heads, this idea caught their attention and stayed with them.

For some participants, the idea came to them well-formed and quickly. For others it emerged gradually and took shape over time. The ideas also came to the participants in different ways, such as through reflection, study, or suggestions from others.

In a few cases, the vision was a reaction to a situation or event they experienced earlier in their lives. Christianna Hang's and Stan Appelbaum's visions came out of experiences they had as young children. As children they were powerless to address the causes of their difficulties. The kernel of their ideas developed during their early life but lay dormant. When they became adults and were in a position to take action, they recalled their childhood experiences and used them to guide the creation of their ideas.

Christianna Hang knew she wanted to provide Hmong students a positive educational experience long before the specific idea to create a charter school came to her. Her own experiences in school led to a vision of operating a school that would offer students a more positive experience than her own. The concept of a charter school was planted in the fertile soil of her greater purpose and she was motivated to pursue it because it was the realization of her vision.

Stan Appelbaum knew from his experiences in the child welfare system that something should and could be done to help children in that system. His vision of enriching the lives of foster children stayed with him and was realized when he founded an organization that addressed the needs of children in foster care.

For others, the source of the idea was a personal realization that they needed to change in order to realize their visions. Thoughtfully reflecting and ruminating caused the idea to emerge. For example, Jim Earley recalled his experience:

> At one point I just knew this isn't how I should
> be spending my life. I had no clue what I should
> be doing, but I knew where I was, wasn't it.

Jim Earley's vision was to align his work with his purpose in life. The idea of creating his own coaching practice came as a result of searching for a way to achieve his vision. When the thought to become a professional coach came to him, he accepted it because he saw it as a way to achieve his vision, even though the notion of operating his own business was intimidating.

Bill and Nancy Lascheid created the framework for their idea, a medical clinic to serve the working poor with dignity and compassionate care, in a relative flash. The idea came to them quickly because they had been serving people in need of health care all their lives. They knew that providing help for those in need was something they wanted to do. The concept of the clinic was accepted and expanded because it was a way to fulfill their vision of providing quality health care to the working poor.

Sona Mehring saw the critical need to connect with family and friends during a time of crisis through the experience of her friends. Her desire to help them, and her knowledge and love of technology enabled her to address her friends' needs quickly. She saw the power of this one website, and the concept for CaringBridge was born.

The idea to create their own companies also came quickly to Justin Griep and Bernie Reisberg when they were presented the opportunity to do so. They had both considered this option early in their lives. It was something they always thought they would do. Bernie had grown up as the third generation of self-made entrepreneurs and when presented a chance to start his own venture, he jumped at it.

Justin vicariously experienced the fun and challenge of starting a new company as he watched his mentor create a business. The mentor shared with Justin the satisfaction he felt at seeing his company take shape. The experience of watching an entrepreneur in action helped clarify Justin's vision of someday being an entrepreneur himself. Later, when the opportunity to form a company that used his skills and expertise presented itself, Justin saw it as a way to realize his vision of becoming an entrepreneur. The original exposure to the concept of entrepreneurship came from his mentor and actually starting his own company became Justin's vision. "I've got to credit having been with this entrepreneur and caught the bug. . . .When I had the opportunity . . . It seemed like the logical next step. Let's go ahead and form a company."

For others the idea evolved gradually. For example, Charlie and Maria Girsch didn't have a lightning bolt experience that told them it was time to start a new business. Rather, they became aware over time that their way of earning a living was going to have to change. Like Jim Earley, Charlie and Maria wanted their jobs to align with their values and to have an integrated life.

> I think it was a reinventing thing. I don't think we just woke up and said, "Let's do this." I'd say as the years went on, you think about what do we do next and of course if you can do something sort of related to [what you know], as opposed to opening an automotive repair shop or something. . . .It was like the world was changing, so you figure out how you become a part of it again.

Sister Jean Thuerauf was focusing on her ministry. Creating a bakery was not even on the horizon when she began inviting children into her home to bake cookies. As the cookie production from her own kitchen expanded and the children to whom she was ministering became teenagers, she saw ways to tie her desire to provide a positive environment for "her kids" to creating a bakery that would employ at-risk youth. "I didn't have any idea about starting a business or the Cookie Cart. It was just what I did to serve the kids. It just evolved because of the mission."

Visions also came from learning or knowing about an issue, hearing something from a colleague, or from other external sources. For example, Ken Miller was aware of the human suffering that the absence of drinkable water was causing in certain areas of the world. Through his work and contacts with others, he knew that technology existed to address this situation. Ken knew other organizations were interested in working on this issue. He was able to take all this information and turn it into a strategic goal for Water For People. This organization was a method for achieving his vision of providing clean water to help keep children healthy.

Dick and Florence Nogaj learned of the needs of a farming community in a newspaper article. Further research made them aware of the much broader issue, which they saw as a crisis in the agricultural business. Dick spoke with experts in the field, did extensive reading, and then clarified his vision to provide an answer to this problem. Thus he and Florence realized that addressing the needs of farm workers could be a way of creating their desired future, which was to make significant contributions to creating positive, prosperous communities.

Key Points about Vision

- You need a distinct, desired future outcome in mind. I call this *Vision*, but it can also be referred to as life's mission or purpose. Regardless of what you call it, the important thing is that you have a clear picture of the desired future you want to create.

▲

- The vision may become evident quickly or emerge over time.

▲

- The source of the vision can be from one's own personal experience, or from an external source. For example, both Stan Appelbuam and Ken Miller sought to improve the lives of children. In Stan's case, his own experience as a foster child fueled his desire to help children in the foster care system. Ken Miller learned that internationally 6,000 – 8,000 children died every day from water-borne illness and that caused him to dedicate his life to bringing potable water to communities throughout the world.

▲

- The details of the vision and the method to achieve the vision may not be evident initially.

▲

- Fulfilling this vision should be seen as something you are destined to do—it is that compelling.

Worksheets

I developed worksheets to help you with the process of bringing your idea to life. These forms are based on what I discovered from people who successfully realized their dreams. But forms don't drive the process. You have to do that. Worksheets can help keep you organized and they may help you think about details or steps in the process, but you're the engine and need to keep things on track. Some people may find the worksheets helpful. Others may ignore them. I offer them as part of this book as an aid for those seeking to bring their ideas to life.

Vision Worksheet Part 1

"Vision" is the word used to describe your desired future. Ask yourself the following questions. Jot down your answers. Your answers will help you clarify your vision and begin building a path to your future.

Who am I?

1. What are my strengths?
2. What do other people say I do well? What compliments or recognition do I get from other people?
3. What accomplishments bring me a sense of satisfaction?
4. What have I done that I felt I did well and really enjoyed doing?
5. What do I enjoy doing so much that I lose track of time when I'm doing it?
6. What do I feel driven to do?
7. What lights up my life? What is my passion?
8. What values do I hold true to no matter what?
9. When I get excited because I will be doing some activity, what is the activity I look forward to doing?
10. What's my purpose in life?

Briefly describe yourself as you are today

What do I want my future to be?

1. What is one thing on my "bucket" list that I **really** want to do?
2. What is something I've wanted to do for a long time that I keep putting off?
3. When I daydream, what comes to my mind? How do I see myself in my dreams?
4. If I could snap my fingers and do anything I wanted, what would that be?
5. What were my goals when I was younger? What did I think I would have done by now, that I still want to do?
6. What have I told good friends/family that I want to accomplish?
7. When I'm older, what will I regret not having done when I had the chance?
8. When I reach the end of my life, what do I want to be able to say I've accomplished?
9. When I have passed on, what do I want other people to remember me for?

Briefly describe who you want to be in the future.

Based on who you are today, and who you want to be, draft a vision statement for yourself.

What are the first steps you need to take to move yourself from where you are to where you want to be?

Vision Worksheet Part 2

Life Line: The line in the middle represents your life. It starts at the top with your birth and ends at the bottom with your death. Mark an "**X**" where you think you are now. In the left column, write down your accomplishments to date. In the right column, write down things you still want to accomplish. Draw a line from each future accomplishment to the place on your life line that indicates when you expect to accomplish it. It's hard to face the fact that we are all finite and won't go on forever. Make the most of the time you have by doing what you love and love what you are doing. Move what you want to accomplish from your "wish list" to your "to do" list. Wanting something to happen isn't the same thing as scheduling something to happen.

Accomplishments to date	Life Line	What I want to accomplish
	Birth	
	●	
	│	
	│	
	│	
	│	
	│	
	│	
	●	
	Death	

Whether you are trying to mobilize a crowd in the grandstand or one person in the office, to Enlist Others you must act on these two essentials:

- *Appeal to common ideals*
- *Animate the vision*

(J. Kouze & B. Posner, 2012)

5

Engaging Others

▲

This theme refers to the participants' ability to recognize the need to involve other people and also be able to entice others to participate in the creation of their dreams. Engaging others involves two distinct elements:

1. **Knowing who needs to be involved with your project**. The involvement might be to secure approvals, meet legal requirements, provide knowledge or services, act as a sounding board, provide a shoulder to lean on—needs you can't fulfill yourself to bring your idea to life.

2. **Taking steps to get others' involved.** This requires deliberate action to successfully secure the necessary support or cooperation and to have others play their essential part in helping achieve your desired goal.

All the visionaries profiled in this book needed some kind of help from others to achieve their idea. Providing this help meant that those who were asked for assistance had to take on additional responsibilities and sometimes do unpleasant tasks; like chasing vermin from an abandoned building, as was the case for those who helped Sister Jean get the building ready for the Cookie Cart. Sometimes these helpers had to do things they had never done before. For many, their help took the form of providing moral support, and just being a friend. Helpers of all kinds had to be engaged in the fulfillment of the participants' visions.

Some cases required help and support from the person's network of friends, or from family members. In such cases, the participants started with a trusting relationship and often just had to make the request and the help was given. However, each participant also had to reach out to strangers, and had to gain the trust of those being asked to help.

Many of the ideas required approval from regulatory authorities. The participants had to understand who had the authority to grant approvals for what, or who needed to be told about what. The participants sought to work collaboratively with those who had regulatory control so that such individuals would be positively disposed to approve the project.

For example, Christianna Hang knew she would never realize her idea of creating Hmong College Prep Academy if she couldn't get others involved in the process. She needed to attract others to her idea so they would play an active part in the creation of the school. She also recognized the need for approval from a variety of officials to be able to open the school. Christianna learned how to approach different individuals to get them engaged. She also was able to gain the support of those in government who needed to approve the creation of the charter school by providing them the information they requested in the manner that they wanted to receive it, and had all her "ducks" neatly in a row. She made it as easy as possible for them by removing potential obstacles in processing her paperwork.

Dick Nogaj engaged academics who helped him learn about agriculture so that he could be successful in creating a viable farming operation. Dick also needed to engage those in a position to provide the permits and approvals needed to operate the farm and open Jubilation, the affordable housing community offered to farm workers. In addition, he needed to convince investors and bankers, who usually made decisions based on hard facts and numbers, that his enterprise was worthy of their support.

Stan Appelbaum first turned to his friends and acquaintances to begin work on making his idea of helping children in foster care into the Foster Care Council of Southwest Florida. "I knew I needed people to work with me and I had some very close friends who worked with me in my human rights work. I said, 'Guys I need your help.'"

Like Christianna Hang and Dick Nogaj, Stan Appelbaum also recognized that he needed cooperation and approval from several individuals and groups in order to realize his vision. In addition, he recognized the need to engage volunteers.

> I work with nothing but volunteers and I get them to do things that I never thought they could do. I try to encourage, help, train, but I back away. I give them room. That is what it takes. You have got to give them the right to express themselves and grow.

Stan also developed an approach to encourage donations. He said that most people feel an affinity to helping children. To build off this positive orientation toward helping children, he emphasized that his organization enriched the lives of children who were not given the opportunities afforded most kids.

Sister Jean Thuerauf was a master at engaging others. She once said, "Who can say 'No' to a nun who is asking for help for children!" She used her connections with people from other parts of the city to serve the needs of her community and, in doing so, realized her vision.

> I invited all the people from Edina that I knew— I used to be out there. Lots of them came over and they came to the bakery, not only to buy cookies but to be with the kids. A little bit of exposure led to a lot of exposure and so we got some sponsors. Before long we had business people helping us and they would see the teenagers working in there and feel good about what they were doing. We were the only thing on our street that had anything positive going on there and lots more people wanted to help.

Part of the skill of engaging others was recognizing whose help was needed. Bill and Nancy Lascheid knew that to open and operate a clinic they needed several other people with specific skills and experience to become involved.

> We then listed all of the professions that we needed to execute this. We made a list of all the names of people with whom we had served on various committees and who had the passion and fire in their belly that we had for the poor and we called the first person on each of the lists. We had a CPA, an attorney, a mental health worker, a fund raiser who was prominent in the area, nurses,

pharmacists, and we called the first one on each
list and we invited them to our house.

Some of the participants effectively used their network of
associates to help bring their idea to fruition. Jim Earley recognized the need to engage others, because initially he had
no idea how to create his own business. He used his network
of friends and acquaintances, not only to learn the rudiments
of opening a business, but also to provide him with opportunities to market his services in ways he found acceptable and
effective. Maria and Charlie Girsch relied on their network
to help them experiment with different approaches as they
developed their training and consulting business.

When Sona Mehring started CaringBridge, she was initially able to rely on help and assistance just from her personal and professional network. However, as the organization
grew, she recognized the need to bring in additional talent so
that the organization could grow and prosper.

Mentors played a significant role for some of the participants. Justin Griep developed a positive relationship with his
mentor, who helped him learn valuable lessons about building a business. Bernie Reisberg was also given guidance by
mentors. Both felt that their relationship with their mentors
was part of why they were successful. Working with a mentor
and using a network of colleagues were common experiences
that helped these participants achieve their visions.

Another example of recognizing the need to involve others
came from Jack Mannion, "I knew that I could only do so much
by myself. But if I worked with organizations and other people,
then I could extend my influence in whatever field I got into
because you link up with other people of like interest."

Key Points about Engaging Others

- Recognize that no matter what idea you want to bring to life, you cannot do it alone. You will need approval or help from someone.

▲

- Identify any approvals you will need from local, state, national or international entities and learn what you need to do to secure their approval.

▲

- Don't be intimidated if the approvals seem beyond reach. Remember, Nancy and Bill Lascheid were able to move the Florida state legislature to get the approvals they needed to set up a clinic.

▲

- Start by engaging your friends and/or family. Whether or not they can provide any of the talent or services you need, you will also need their emotional support.

▲

- Develop specific strategies to secure help from the people who can provide what you need. Approach each as an individual. Don't expect everyone to respond to the same message in the same way. Tailor your approach to fit the motivation, aspirations and style of the person whose help you are seeking.

Engaging Others Worksheet

This worksheet will help you identify who you need to involve in the process of bringing your idea to life, why you need their involvement, and what strategies you will use to secure what you need from them.

First determine whose help you will need. You may add names to this list throughout the course of bringing your idea to life. Sometimes you will have a specific name. Other times you will have the name of the group, board, municipality, etc. and part of your task will be to determine who specifically you need to contact to secure what you need from that group.

Having the names and contact information of all those from whom you need help in one place will keep you organized and make retrieving this information easier.

Before contacting people, be clear as to the type of help you need. Be able to explain why you need their help. Draft your request in writing and review it before sending, even if it is just an email. Rehearse your message before approaching someone in person or by phone.

Develop a strategy for each person. Sometimes it may be as simple as directly approaching a good friend, telling that person about your idea and asking for help. In other cases, you may use a social network to find a person who can provide you something essential. You should think about how you will present your idea in a way that will appeal to a specific individual. Don't just leave the strategy to chance.

The notes section on this form is a place for you to record when and how you have approached people, their reactions, and other relevant information.

Remember, forms don't drive the process, but they may help keep it organized.

Engaging Others Worksheet

Name	Contact Info	What I Need	Strategy

Notes

Name	Contact Info	What I Need	Strategy

Notes

Name	Contact Info	What I Need	Strategy

Notes

Name	Contact Info	What I Need	Strategy

Notes

Name	Contact Info	What I Need	Strategy

Notes

Write your goals in concrete
and your plans in sand.

Anonymous

6

Flexible Processes and Plans

▲

Defined plans and processes facilitated the realization of the participants' ideas. However, these plans and processes were not so rigid that the participants followed them at the expense of losing sight of the ultimate goal. Their plans and approaches had to be modified as they encountered obstacles or as new and more promising opportunities presented themselves.

The time spent on planning and the amount of detail in the plan varied by individual participant. Some participants were very organized and developed detailed strategies about how they would proceed from ideation to implementation. Others had much less detail with only vague ideas about how they would take their journey. However, regardless of the sophistication of the initial plan, all participants employed a flexible process that allowed them to modify their approach as they encountered unforeseen obstacles or opportunities.

The participants were willing to explore alternative approaches so that they could achieve their vision. In this study, *flexible* refers to the ability to adapt to new, different, or changing requirements (Merriam-Webster Collegiate Dictionary, 2004). Flexibility is distinguished from being resourceful, another sub-theme identified in this study. *Resourceful* refers to being a good problem solver and finding alternative ways to proceed. Flexibility, on the other hand, was the willingness to pursue these alternatives, to take a different path. Flexibility allowed the participants to respond to new circumstances and change approaches, but does not imply that their visions changed. The vision remained consistent while the plan and processes to achieve it were modified as needed to increase the probability of achieving the vision.

Many of the ideas evolved over time and thus it was necessary for participants to respond to changing situations or to adapt based on new knowledge. A flexible process allowed the participants to abandon strategies that weren't as effective in favor of others that were more likely to lead to implementation of their idea.

For example, Jim Earley realized that the kind of work he was doing—a safe and secure position in a large corporation—was not what he wanted to do and that coaching was to be his life's work. His first thought was to find a company that would hire him as a coach. A brief investigation made him realize that being hired by a company to be a coach was highly unlikely. If he wanted to pursue coaching, he would have to start his own business. The realization that he would be in business for himself, instead of working for someone else as he had always done, caused a complete change in his mindset regarding work. His ability to make this change demonstrated flexibility in his approach to achieving his vision.

Another way Jim Earley used a flexible process was the way he approached necessary tasks he didn't want to do. Jim knew himself well enough to recognize that if he did not want to do something, it would not get done. To ensure he accomplished necessary tasks, he found ways to "want" to do things. For example, he knew he needed a system to stay in touch with his current and potential clients, but he didn't like the idea of calling them on a regular basis. He also abhorred "cold calling" potential clients, and his initial attempts to do so had not been fruitful. All the "experts" told him that calls were the way to build and maintain his business. Client contact was a part of his business he felt he had to do, but the process of making a list of who to call each day, some of them cold calls, and then making these calls was neither comfortable for him, nor was it effective.

He was intrigued by recently released software that would take care of sending emails to current and potential clients on a regular basis and would remind him who he needed to call each week. Instead of spending his time making lists, or fretting about calls he didn't want to make, he devoted his attention to programming the software. Tinkering with technology was something he did enjoy, and so he found not only greater contentment in doing necessary tasks, but also he experienced better results. Using a flexible process to achieve his goals allowed Jim to pursue what needed to be done rather than abandon his goal because the "standard" method wasn't something he wanted to do.

Although Jim planned various parts of his transition from working for an organization to having his own business, he didn't have an overall umbrella plan that guided the entire process. "For me, the process of moving from the corporate world to my own business was serendipity after serendipity after serendipity, and I just let it happen."

Sona Mehring was flexible in her approach regarding CaringBridge. It initially seemed like something she would do "on the side," sort of a hobby. Then she realized the potential for what CaringBridge offered and she knew it would need her full time attention. Her next adjustment was to set up the organization as a non-profit, helping to ensure that the vital services of CaringBridge could be offered to those who needed them free of charge.

Justin Griep thought he would provide basic computer skills for clients. He found that his clients needed more services than he initially thought. To improve the likelihood of success for his company, and to meet the needs of his clients, he had to expand his services. This required him to increase his own knowledge and figure out ways to offer the services his clients wanted. "So now, we've switched business models. We actually try to put something to the bottom line rather than just . . . make sure your computers work."

Bernie Reisberg demonstrated his flexibility when he realized that his first adventure in business, importing art, was not going to be sustainable. He quickly changed his business model, and jumped on an opportunity to create a manufacturing business.

After a few years, he again restructured his business model as market conditions required he do things differently to remain viable. Even though the buzz word from the "experts" was "Focus, focus," and the advice they gave was "Stick with what you've got," Bernie realized that the better course for him was to offer as many different products as he could to as many different audiences as possible. Being flexible and able to respond to changes in the business environment has allowed Bernie to get through some of the most difficult economic times since the Great Depression. He kept the vision of owning his own business alive, while changing "exactly what we do and who we do it for." Bernie isn't thrown by situations that make his original plan unworkable. "So you deal with problems as they come . . .You just have to take care of it so you can move from point A to B to C."

Charlie and Maria Girsch also realized the need for flexible processes as they brought Creativity Central to life. Their original assumptions about how they should proceed proved ineffective.

> I would like to point out one thing we thought was going to be true and that we found we were totally wrong. [They thought] What we'll really do is ideation because we are so good at that and it will be the major part of our business with giving an occasional talk. Guess what? It was just the opposite! The amount of ideation we have done is not proportionate to the amount of talks.

They saw the need to change their direction and find another way to deliver their services. Maria Girsch said that one of the lessons she learned from this experience is the "need to detach [from] a specific outcome." She added, "It is all right to have an outcome in mind, but you need to see where it goes and be ready to change directions as needed to accomplish your goal." Charlie Girsch expressed this ability to change by saying, "We had a lot of flexibility. We just have an uncanny ability to fly with things. We don't have to be tied down."

When forming the entity that would eventually be Water For People, Jack Mannion and Ken Miller tried a number of different approaches before finally finding a model that worked and was accepted by the appropriate authorities.

> We did another spin-off . . . that didn't work. A couple of the things that I've been involved with either succeeded for a while and then failed or didn't work at all. You learn and then you try

something else . . . and you keep building. (J. Mannion)

Bill and Nancy Lascheid needed flexible processes because they had not anticipated the amount of support they would receive or the size of the clinic they could create. Referring to the two very generous donations they received that funded their new clinic, Nancy said, "I mean we had the plan but it [was] Bill and me down in those three rooms . . . so getting something as grandiose as this certainly wasn't in our plan." To take advantage of the opportunities presented them, Nancy and Bill modified their approach and adapted their plan.

Florence and Dick Nogaj demonstrated their ability to flex their plans and processes by the way they reacted when the hurricane forced the closing of the Harvest for Humanity farm. They turned their attention to other endeavors, such as operating an office building that offers space for non-profits. Farming and office buildings are very different, but each allows them to continue fulfilling their vision of making the world a better place.

Key Points about Flexible Processes and Plans

- The "plan" is not a dictator. Don't do anything just because it is in the plan. Your actions need to make sense. Be willing to explore alternative approaches to achieve your vision.

▲

- Keep processes flexible to allow yourself to abandon those that are not as effective as they might be. Explore other ways that may be more likely to lead to implementation of your idea.

▲

- Be ready to jump on opportunities as they present themselves. Eye on the vision. Ear to the ground. Body in motion. (Think of it as a sort of Twister game gone amok!)

▲

- Throughout your process of bringing your idea to life, ask, "Could there be a better way?" And be ready to answer "Yes."

▲

- Remember, there are many different paths that can reach the end of the rainbow.

Flexible Plans and Processes Worksheet

This worksheet will help you build flexibility into your planning process. It's easier to adapt if you have thought about some of the challenges you might face that will require you to change your plans.

For each key step you anticipate in bringing your idea to life, think about what might get in the way; what might prevent you from doing what you want. Then consider ways you can remove, or overcome these obstacles. Finally, it is always good to have a "Plan B"—another option that will move you forward if you find you can't overcome a specific obstacle.

Key Step in Process	What Obstacle Might Be in the Way?	How Can I Overcome This Obstacle?	What Is My Plan B?

Unless commitment is made, there are only promises and hopes...but no plans.

Peter Drucker

7

Commitment

▲

A common experience for all participants was their strong commitment to implementing their ideas. I created a formula that I think describes commitment. Commitment is the product of tenacity and resourcefulness, thus:

Commitment = Tenacity X Resourcefulness

Like any multiplication problem, if either multiplier (in this case, tenacity and resourcefulness are the multipliers) is zero, the final product will be zero. I don't include this formula to challenge your math skills (mine are rather dusty and inept from non-use), but understanding that these two factors need each other to create commitment is the crux of the issue. A simple formula seems to make the point. Tenacity and resourcefulness enhance each other, but the absence of either will make true commitment impossible to achieve.

Commitment refers to the level of dedication and sense of responsibility attached to achieving a goal. Commitment is more intense than mere support of an idea. It goes beyond simple desire or wanting a result. It involves aligning action and decisions with the achievement of the goal. The participants' commitment was so strong and pervasive that it drove their behavior and decisions. For some, it caused them to make significant changes in their lifestyles and do things they had never thought they would do.

Commitment requires an acceptance that one's think-ing and behavior may have to adjust to achieve the goal. Changing habits and thinking processes is not an easy under-taking. Therefore, true commitment is rare. Dick and Florence Nogaj changed the direction of their lives to commit them-selves to the development of their vision. They abandoned other pursuits and focused attention and resources on bring-ing their idea of a fair wage farm and housing community to reality. They moved to a part of Florida where they had never lived, learned about an industry in which they had no experi-ence, and took on new responsibilities—all to achieve the vi-sion they had identified. "So we made a commitment . . . to take this journey" (D. Nogaj).

Dick and Florence Nogaj were recognized as committed to a vision by many in the community. They demonstrated their sense of responsibility for seeing the project through to completion by developing relationships in the community, taking on personal debt, and working long hours. As one reporter noted, "With their committed efforts, the Nogajs are changing the face of Immokalee and serving as living exam-ples of what not taking no for an answer can do to transform a community" (Sparks, 2004).

Jim Earley demonstrated his commitment to creating his vision when he took on responsibility for starting his own busi-ness, and in the process, modifying his lifestyle to do so. He described the feeling of commitment he had when he start-ed his journey from secure, but unfulfilling employment in a stable position at a prosperous company to being a fledgling independent business owner. He told himself, "There was no escape clause. There was no way out. . . . Here's the funda-mental thing. I set myself on finding my life's work, and then I decided I had found it." He indicated that once he found the way to achieve his vision, he was totally committed to doing whatever was needed to live it.

Jim described himself as an introvert who shied away from anything like marketing or public speaking. However, he realized the need to perform such tasks in order to get his business started. One evening when he was attending a dinner for a professional association, he was given an impromptu opportunity to speak about his new business to a large audience of potential customers. As an introverted reflective thinker, speaking to a group of strangers off the cuff was one of his worst nightmares. He realized that this was an opportunity he should not pass up. His commitment to living his vision spurred him on. "It's setting your commitment level. If you decide this is the one, then okay - end of story."

Justin Griep was committed to achieving his vision. He described himself as "driven." When asked about his personal characteristics he indicated that he was "committed," and said, "I like to take a vision—my dream and make it a reality."

Some participants used the word "passionate" to describe their level of commitment to bringing their idea to life. Speaking about the key trait he saw in himself that enabled him to realize his idea, Stan Appelbaum said,

> I'm passionate. You have to be passionate in anything you want to do. You have to create a passion for it. You have to have enough reason to do it so that it energizes you, encompasses all of your abilities to create something that is difficult to create. It is not easy to create a non-profit from scratch and it is certainly difficult to go out and raise hundreds of thousands of dollars in funds. But it can be done and you don't have to be rich to do it. You just have to have a passion for it.

Christianna Hang also described herself as passionate and committed. "I am very passionate and dedicated to my work . . .I believe people see me as very dedicated and hard working." Sometimes her dedication to her work got in the way of spending time with her family. She regretted this, but her commitment to fulfilling her vision gave her perspective when trying to balance all the important parts of her life.

> You have to be willing to sacrifice every minute of your time. . . .Sometimes I almost put my work in front of my family because it [creating her vision] will help not only my children but also help the world. I want to be able to look at my family and say that if I have neglected them it was for a good purpose. For me this school is a dream come true.

Nancy Lascheid said that she and her husband had been passionate about helping the poor. One of the factors they considered when looking for others to join them in implementing their idea was their level of commitment, because they saw that as "an essential characteristic to get things done." Also, they demonstrated their commitment when they established an ambitious timeline for opening their clinic. They felt they had a short window of opportunity when the community, government, and their colleagues could all come together to create their vision of a clinic that served the working poor. "If we didn't make a commitment, we were never going to do it." Through their efforts, the clinic opened on time.

Tenacity

The participants in this study stayed with the idea in pursuit of their vision and did not waiver in their commitment.

They successfully brought their ideas to life. In this study, *tenacity* refers to being very determined and not easily swayed from an objective. It means having fortitude to endure hardships and challenges in the process of pursuing a goal. Tenacity means never giving up and continuing to try even in the face of adversity. Csikszentmihalyi, a recognized expert on creativity, conveyed the importance of tenacity, "A genuinely creative accomplishment is almost never the result of a sudden insight, a light bulb flashing on in the dark, but comes after years of hard work" (1996, p. 1).

Several of the participants used the word "tenacious" when asked to describe their characteristics or traits. Nancy Lascheid called herself "determined" and said she was "not intimidated by the magnitude of something. I just do what I have to do." Similarly, Stan Appelbaum described himself as "stubborn" and that "I didn't know how to quit."

Dick Nogaj commented on tenacity while creating Harvest for Humanity and Jubilation, "We were tenacious and persuasive to the point where we never took no for an answer." Various local newspaper articles reported the progress of Dick's idea as it was being realized. One article written about Dick included the following:

> He never gave up on the idea, even though he had many hurdles to clear such as finding the right crop that would grow in the area and offer high enough prices to sustain fair farm wages, getting support from a university and local financiers, and all the other challenges inherent to starting an agricultural business and housing community. Dick Nogaj faced many challenges and the work consumed a lot of personal

time and effort, but the vision became a reality (Sparks, August 2004).

Bernie Reisberg also enjoyed the challenges he faced implementing his idea and was tenacious in the pursuit of his vision. He said he had a pretty simple philosophy, "If you don't quit, you can't lose. We've come this far. We have to keep going. And I don't think about that a lot. I go through the motions each day and I do what I have to do."

Christianna Hang experienced resistance from the government, the educational community, and even from some in her own ethnic community, but she tenaciously pursued her idea to create a charter school until it was a reality. She said her philosophy was that "Failure was not an option" and that she "was going to do this! You have to have courage. Believe in this thing; that it *will* happen if you don't give up, no matter how hard it is."

Justin Griep described how he and his business partner had been tenacious in the face of difficulties and very limited income. They struggled for many months while their clients were late with payments and new work wasn't coming to them. "We went through all of that, but we knew we had to do it. We stuck in there and then the money started flowing again."

Resourcefulness

The participants in this study demonstrated the ability to find what was needed to achieve their ideas. They were resourceful in discovering ways to accomplish the vision. *Resourcefulness* means being able to meet the demands of situations as they presented themselves—to be able to devise ways and means (Merriam-Webster Collegiate Dictionary,

2004). Resourceful individuals are ingenious and enterprising. They deal effectively with problems or difficulties. Those who are resourceful are inventive, creative, and capable of finding alternative methods to achieve their goals.

In seeking alternatives, participants made use not only of their own talents and resources but also those of family, friends, acquaintances, and strangers to overcome obstacles and to continue to move forward.

They were able to find alternatives to solve problems, even in difficult circumstances. For example, Nancy and Bill Lascheid realized that in order to open a clinic to serve the working poor, they would need doctors willing to volunteer their time. One of the greatest obstacles to getting physicians to donate their services was the need for them to be covered by malpractice insurance. It was impossible for the clinic to provide such coverage, and it was equally impossible for doctors to practice without the protection of medical malpractice insurance. The standard model, whereby a clinic or practice group provides access to insurance, would not work. The Lascheids were undaunted by what seemed to many others an unsolvable problem. Being resourceful, they pursued the creative solution of working with the government to provide sovereign immunity to doctors while they worked in the clinic. It was a new approach and required legislative action, but their resourcefulness allowed the Lascheids to approach this problem in a creative way and find a unique solution.

Christianna Hang recognized that as a young woman, she wouldn't be as persuasive as other members of the Hmong community when trying to encourage parents to enroll their children in Hmong Academy. She had gotten legal approval for the school, and she could even see how to get the necessary staff, but she needed students to enroll. The common methods of attracting students to a new school were to announce the creation of a new charter school through press releases and to plaster flyers in the immediate neighborhood. However, such methods wouldn't serve her purpose. To convince parents that they could trust this new school, she persuaded the elders of the Hmong community to speak on her behalf. She had to use this resource as a means to solve her problem. She collaborated with Hmong leaders to educate parents about the potential benefits of the school, and to contact Hmong families individually.

Sister Jean demonstrated her resourcefulness when she faced a variety of problems associated with starting the Cookie Cart. She found ingenious ways to acquire the building and equipment she needed to get started. Whenever faced with the need for specific equipment, supplies or people, she found unique ways to obtain them, thus allowing her to continue the pursuit of her vision.

When creating Water For People, Ken Miller recognized that other agencies had tried to improve the sanitary conditions and provide clean water to various parts of the world, but none of the projects were sustained over time. Instead of following the prevailing practices, Ken and others at Water For People used their ingenuity and developed a new model which required commitment from the community being served, training for local workers and residents, and sustained support until the local people were ready to take over managing the project. They used the resources available at the site to develop an approach that resulted in a sustainable project.

Jim Earley found ways to overcome personal obstacles such as his reluctance to sell his services. He reflected about how he faced the dilemma of knowing he had to sell his services, yet nearly panicking at the thought of doing marketing in traditional ways.

> What I was doing looked and felt impossible. I considered myself one of the great introverts of the Western Hemisphere. And I needed to go tell people that they should hire me. Or I needed to somehow get in front of people so that they might hire me. I just went around in a circle— Ohhh, I don't think I can do this. What should I do? Well, this is your life's work, and ya know, you get to go first. Well okay. I guess I'll try something else! I don't have to make cold calls. . . .My best suit is one-to-one conversations and I know a lot of people. I'll start with them, and business started coming in. I solved my problem.

Several participants saw challenges not as something to be feared, but something to be welcomed as a test of their abilities or their dedication to the idea. Jack Mannion saw dealing effectively with challenges as an important factor in individual and organizational success. "So the question is, when you meet an obstacle, what can you do to circumvent it? And that's part of the fun, the challenge."

Maria and Charlie Girsch had honed their resourcefulness and creativity during the years they spent as successful toy inventors. They applied these same skills to the challenge of realizing their vision of creating a company that provided creativity training and services to clients. They used their talents for innovation and found ways to apply them in a different field. Thus, they solved their dilemma of finding a way to stay connected to creativity that also provided an income.

Key Points about Commitment

- Commitment requires more than just wanting something. Ask yourself if you are really ready to change your behavior and your pattern of thinking in order to bring your idea to life. If you aren't willing to do so, you aren't committed. Find another idea that you can commit to.

▲

- Be ready to be told "no" and instead of thinking, "Ok, so I can't," think, "I need to find another way."

▲

- Think about getting what you need from a variety of sources so that if one doesn't work out, you have others to consider.

▲

- Don't expect everyone else to embrace your idea initially. Stick with it. Be tenacious. Take the example of Christianna Hang who initially couldn't get support from the State of Minnesota, other educators or her own community, but she prevailed.

▲

- Follow the wisdom of Woodrow Wilson who said, "I not only use all the brains I have, but all those I can borrow."

Commitment Worksheet

Compute your commitment score by rating your tenacity and resourcefulness. Circle the number, 0 – 5, with 0 = *Not at all like me*, 5 = *Very much like me*, that best describes you related to each statement.

Total your score for tenacity and for resourcefulness. Multiply these two numbers. This is your commitment score. The higher the score, the greater your level of commitment. Remember, since you are multiplying these numbers, if either tenacity or resourcefulness is 0, your commitment score will be zero.

Tenacity	Resourcefulness
When I start something, I finish it. 0 1 2 3 4 5	I can find multiple solutions to a problem. 0 1 2 3 4 5
When I face a challenge, I'm energized to meet it. 0 1 2 3 4 5	I may not know the answer, but I know where to find it. 0 1 2 3 4 5
I am persistent. 0 1 2 3 4 5	I find ways to use what I have to do what I need to get done. 0 1 2 3 4 5
People call me determined. 0 1 2 3 4 5	People say I'm creative. 0 1 2 3 4 5
I don't give up easily. 0 1 2 3 4 5	I like considering alternatives. 0 1 2 3 4 5
I don't take NO for an answer. 0 1 2 3 4 5	I'm good at brainstorming. 0 1 2 3 4 5
I can be stubborn. 0 1 2 3 4 5	I like to do familiar things in different ways. 0 1 2 3 4 5
Total (T)	Total (R)
T ( ) X R ( ) = ( ) Commitment Score	

*Attitude is a little thing that
makes a big difference.*

Winston Churchill

8

Positive Attitude

▲

The participants believed in the possibility of a positive out-come and kept faith that they would be successful in the pur-suit of their vision. Those who are optimistic and focus on potential benefits are considered to have a positive attitude. It is seeing the glass as half-full, not half-empty. A positive attitude focuses the person's attention on the possible rather than keeping attention on the problem. It is not a naïve and untested view of reality, but rather a hopeful view of the fu-ture and seeing the potential for a positive outcome.

Having a positive attitude makes life more enjoyable. Energy is focused on accomplishing things, and not wasted on fretting. Positivity helps you live in the moment and not dwell on past failures or fear future challenges. It is the ability to enjoy whatever one is doing, even if it is "work."

Christianna Hang always saw possibilities. She faced each challenge with the belief that it could be overcome and that there would be a positive result. "No matter how much you think you cannot do something, no matter how discouraged the world gets you . . . if you put your mind into anything you can make it happen." She had a firm belief that good things would happen.

Sona Mehring described herself as having a positive at-titude about life and values "fun, laughter and humor." Sona said that someone once told her, "Jump and the net will appear." She believes that if you follow your passion, positive things will happen.

Maria Girsch talked about the need to have a positive orientation when venturing out on a path that might look risky. She said that she always had faith that things would turn out well. "I just believed that we could do it and we did."

Several of the people profiled in this book described themselves as optimists. Stan Appelbaum said he was an innate optimist and expressed his positive attitude, "I give everybody the benefit of the doubt to begin with because I think people are basically good people. I think this is a marvelous world we live in."

Sister Jean Thuerauf maintained a positive attitude and hope for the future even though she resided in a violent, impoverished community where many lived in despair. She always believed she would get what she needed, in spite of the odds against that happening. People would tell her that she is expecting too much; setting her goals too high. They would tell stories of other times people tried to make significant changes in the neighborhood and were unsuccessful. They talked about the lack of money and other factors inherent in a poor community that contributed to good efforts failing to deliver their desired results. Despite the logic that said something would not happen, she said, "Even when we needed something everyone said we wouldn't get, I just smiled, and stayed positive, and we got what we needed. Isn't that neat!"

Dick and Florence Nogaj remained positive and confident that their idea for an agriculture business and affordable housing could be created, even when many in the community told them it was impossible. At every step in the process they encountered associates who told them to abandon the idea—that it was just not possible. They kept an optimistic outlook and Dick now reflects:

> They said we couldn't do it. We built condo- miniums for the first time for this market and people said, "They will not sell." And of course they sold [all] the homes. They said we couldn't get an [ethnically diverse] community to work together and now it is a well-integrated, diverse community that works!

The participants also displayed a positive orientation by being hopeful about the future. They carried this belief throughout the process of moving their ideas from conception to implementation. As expressed by Bernie Reisberg, "We had aspirations that this was going to work. It never dawned on us that something wasn't going to work."

Justin Griep expressed his positive attitude and belief in possibilities. He said that he has a "strong belief that things are going to work out, even if they don't work out exactly as I expect. . . but there is always a way."

Key Points about Positive Attitude

- When you encounter a setback, don't be derailed. Think of it as a learning experience. Assimilate what is useful and move on.

▲

- Look for the good things in everyday life and take enjoyment from them.

▲

- Surround yourself with positive people. Their enthusiasm can be contagious.

▲

- Find reasons to celebrate small victories as you bring your idea to life. Don't wait until the very end to recognize your achievements. Feed off the energy of small accomplishments to keep going forward.

▲

- Take control of what you can control. You can't always control what happens, but you decide how you will respond.

Positive Attitude Worksheet

Some of us are wired with a more positive attitude than others. If you are blessed with positivity, enjoy! If you sometimes struggle to be positive, if seeing the negative side is easier, don't lose hope. You can change your attitude. The following worksheet offers some suggestions to help stay in, or move to a positive outlook.

Positive Attitude Worksheet Part 1

Put a check in the left column to indicate which actions related to forming and keeping a positive attitude you do on a regular basis. Pick one or two of the items you didn't check, commit to start doing them, and put a check in the far right column for these items. After a month, review and see if you are doing these actions to help support a positive attitude.

I do this	Actions	I will do this
	Use positive words. Avoid, "I can't" and substitute, "I will" or "I'll figure out a way."	
	Embrace the moment. You can't live in the past or the future. You only have this moment. Make the most of it.	
	Be bold. Do something that challenges you.	
	Smile. It is hard to stay mad, depressed or ornery when you smile.	
	Don't compare yourself to the superstars.	
	Appreciate what you have and who you are.	

I do this	Actions	I will do this
	Find people who like to do the same things you do and do these things together regularly.	
	Recognize that you get to make choices. Reduce the number of things you do because you *have* to and do more of the things that you do because you *choose* to.	
	Look good to feel good. Put on your favorite clothes. Get your hair styled. Indulge yourself with a new accessory.	
	Read or watch something inspirational. Avoid programs or articles that bring you down, make you nervous, or create other negative reactions.	
	Avoid spending time with whiners.	
	Ask for help when you need it.	
	Find someone who can use your help and offer your assistance. Volunteer for something that energizes you.	

Positive Attitude Worksheet Part 2

Take a standard sheet of lined paper, or use the worksheet provided here. Start at the top line. Write something positive about yourself—something you do well, a trait you are glad you have, etc. Keep writing until you reach the bottom of the page. Seeing all these positive things about yourself can't help but brighten your attitude.

9

Meaning of the Experience

▲

The participants indicated that bringing an idea from conception to completion had been a growth experience for them. They also reported that they had experienced difficult times during the process. While the experience had not always been "fun," the participants all responded that it had been overwhelmingly positive. Participants indicated they had gained increased confidence and a strong sense of satisfaction from bringing their idea to life.

Increased Confidence

A common reaction, among the participants when asked to describe what the experience meant to them, was that they learned they could do anything if they had confidence they would do it. Several indicated that achieving this idea inspired them to set more far-reaching goals for themselves. Stan Appelbaum said, "I learned that people don't set high enough goals for themselves, that if you have a good idea and you have passion for the idea, you can do anything."

Christianna Hang expressed that opening Hmong College Prep Academy gave her confidence to pursue opportunities to create additional schools.

> I am inspired to a larger goal. I will open a
> network organization that will help start other
> schools. I want this school to be known through-
> out the country—throughout the world—where
> students from other countries can come here
> to study. . .I hope to spread Hmong Academy
> across the country.

Justin Griep indicated that being successful in this endeavor was an important learning experience for him and one
that will enable him to continue to expand his business. He
expressed increased confidence in his ability to continue being a successful entrepreneur.

Bernie Reisberg stated that he had personal pride in seeing what he had been able to create, and that it gave him
faith he would continue to meet the challenges of managing
a business in a changing economy. Dick and Florence Nogaj
saw the realization of their idea to provide livable wages to
farm workers as something they had done to contribute to
society; something that gave them great personal satisfaction
and confidence that such an endeavor could be successful in
other locations.

Jim Earley said that being a coach was his destiny and that
the self-assurance he gained from implementing his idea was
helpful to him as he coached others to pursue their own personal visions. After establishing himself as a personal coach,
he said, "I've never been more confident than now."

Satisfaction From Creating Something New

Several participants in this study created entities that
serve other people. At one level, serving the needs of others is altruistic, and certainly their focus was on providing

help to those in need. In addition, serving the needs of others gave the participants a great sense of personal satisfaction and fulfillment. Stan Appelbaum had been a foster child and knew the challenges children in foster care face. His experience of creating a program that addressed their needs and helped enrich their lives gave him a great sense of satisfaction and accomplishment.

> People don't do anything without getting something out of it. Let's be realistic. I get a lot of recognition, but more importantly, when people ask me why I do something it is because I get something from it. I know when I lay my head down on the pillow at night I need to feel comfortable with who I am. You have to have some feeling for your fellow human being . . . and that makes me feel better about myself.

Dick and Florence Nogaj also felt they benefitted from taking action to help others because such action was consistent with their values. They were described in a local newspaper article as "entrepreneurial philanthropists" (Sparks, 2004). They reported a great sense of personal satisfaction and accomplishment in actually making a difference in the world.

Christianna Hang experienced harassment because of her ethnicity while attending elementary school. This experience stayed in her memory. When, as an adult, she had the opportunity to create a charter school, she realized a great sense of satisfaction that she had done something to spare other children the negative experiences she had endured.

Ken Miller saw the need to provide sanitary conditions and drinkable water to communities throughout the world. He experienced gratification in the creation of Water For

People because he had done something to address an identified and unmet need.

> Before Water For People, all we'd done was pro-
> vide countries with our books and standards.
> Maybe we should outreach to them . . . and we
> did . . . so now it's come a long way and I'm
> proud of what we accomplished.

Jack Mannion, who worked with Ken Miller, also experienced a sense of accomplishment with the realization of their
idea, Water For People.

> It's enormously satisfying. . . Every mark . . . of
> progress; every step forward; every new pla-
> teau it reaches is a level of accomplishment that
> might not have been achieved. I think that it's
> important. Successes like that need to be cele-
> brated. . . There's great satisfaction, I've found,
> in taking something from nothing . . . and then
> going out and doing it.

Another source of satisfaction for some of the participants
in this study was a sense they had created something enduring and repeatable. They weren't seeking a short-term fix
and seeing that the entity they created was sustainable gave
them a sense of fulfillment. Knowing they had created a template others could follow made them proud of what they had
achieved.

Dick Nogaj discovered the numerous and complex problems that existed because farm workers weren't earning a livable wage. He was motivated to do something to not only
improve life for the farm workers, but also to address a serious

issue in American agriculture. He expressed his sense of satisfaction at achieving something that went beyond the limits of the specific entity he created.

> We wanted to develop a new alternative farming model that would pay living wages and that would demonstrate not just an idea or concept, but . . . turn them into reality and . . . be able to make a difference and bring about systemic change; bring about a paradigm shift, which is what we think agriculture badly needs.

Bill and Nancy Lascheid had a feeling of satisfaction from creating a model that demonstrated quality health care could be provided in a respectful and caring manner for those with limited financial resources. They experienced years of frustration working in a healthcare system that seemed unable to tackle difficult issues. The Neighborhood Clinic showed that an alternative to common medical practice was possible.

Given that they were of retirement age, Nancy and Bill took steps to ensure the clinic would continue after they stopped working there. Knowing they had provided for the continuation of the clinic, regardless of their level of personal involvement, gave them a sense of comfort.

Bernie Reisberg articulated his satisfaction at achieving a goal and meeting a challenge. He expressed his personal pride in seeing what he had been able to create. It wasn't just the success of the company that was satisfying, but also knowing he had conquered the challenges he faced to realize his vision.

Some of the participants indicated that the source of their satisfaction came from feeling they had fulfilled their destiny—something they were ordained to do. Jim Earley said being a coach was his destiny. It tied his life, his work, and his way of earning a living together. He had a deep sense of satisfaction because he felt he was following what he was meant to do.

Sona Mehring saw the creation of CaringBridge as a labor of love that allowed her to fulfill her desire to use technology in a way that meets very human needs. She was able to combine her "geeky" side with her compassionate side—both of which she knew were a core part of who she is.

Some participants felt they were doing what God wanted them to do. Sister Jean Thuerauf said that creating the bakery was satisfying because it was all part of God's plan and that she merely followed God's lead. This was the work God intended her to do, and any credit for any accomplishment should go to God. Sister Jean Thuerauf, an individual of deep religious faith, believed that she was being guided by God.

Dick and Florence Nogaj saw the creation of Harvest for Humanity and Jubilation as an opportunity presented to them by a higher power who helped guide them throughout the process. Their experience of creating the fair wage farm and the housing community was not only a trek through an industry in which they had never worked before, in an area of the country where they had not previously lived, but more importantly to them, it was a spiritual journey.

Bill and Nancy Lascheid expressed that they felt a sense of destiny and that what they were doing was what God wanted them to do. They said they didn't think they could have accomplished all they had if God's hand had not been "at the controls."

10

Closing Comments

▲

The participants in this study shared the experience of bringing an idea from conception to implementation. I greatly appreciate the opportunity to have met them and learn their stories. Their examples are an inspiration for me and provide a model for anyone interested in pursuing the realization of a vision.

When I began this study, I had certain assumptions about what I would find. I thought that those who were able to bring their idea to life would:

1. be passionate about their ideas;
2. develop and follow some kind of plan;
3. have readily available resources and,
4. that realizing their idea would engender a sense of accomplishment.

I found some of these assumptions were supported by this research, while others were not. The evidence that emerged from an analysis of the data gathered for this study supported the importance of passion for the idea. It also indicated that being committed to doing whatever was necessary to bring the idea into being was an important element in seeing an idea through to fruition. The study also supported the assumption that realizing their visions would engender a sense of accomplishment.

However, my assumptions regarding planning and easy availability of resources were not consistent factors across participants, and therefore were not supported by this research. The amount and type of planning varied by individual participant. A few, either by personal choice or because the situation required it, took great pains to prepare detailed and careful action plans to guide their processes. In contrast, others had a well thought out vision, but the actual implementation of the idea advanced with a minimal amount of planning. For example, Charlie and Maria Girsch compared their process of developing Creativity Central to an occasion earlier in their lives when they created a more traditional business. For that business they "followed all the rules" and developed detailed business plans. In contrast, Creativity Central was implemented without a formal plan. "But this one was much more slippery. Not in a bad sense, but in the sense that we grew into it" (M. Girsch).

Likewise, my assumption regarding participants having readily available resources was not a common factor. In fact, most had limited resources, and a significant part of their challenge was obtaining what they required. None of the participants created the realization of their vision solely by using their own personal resources. Nonetheless, for all participants, the achievement of their vision became possible because of their ability to secure what they needed.

The themes that emerged from analysis of the data demonstrated the vital role of vision in motivating the participants to pursue their idea. Of the myriad of ideas that crossed their minds, the specific idea studied here was accepted by the participants because it represented a way to achieve a desired future state. All participants had a clear sense of purpose and were motivated to take action to achieve their vision. The vision serves as a beacon, guiding the individual's actions. The purpose must be clear, even if the final result and the precise method of moving from conception to implementation are initially unclear.

A specific idea becomes the focus when it is seen as the vehicle for achieving the desired future—the vision. The person seeking to bring the concept to life feels the compelling pull of the vision, as if being drawn to a powerful magnet. The vision energizes the person to push out of the current state and propels the person down a sometimes bumpy and winding path toward the creation of the entity that embodies the vision.

Another factor important to the phenomenon of bringing an idea to life was to engage others in the process. Participants recognized the need for others to be part of the process of bringing their ideas from conception to fruition. The extent of others' involvement and the roles played by others varied greatly. However, the participants were able to get the support and cooperation they needed to bring their ideas from conception to reality.

Others not only can provide emotional support but also can help in practical, useful ways by sharing their talents. Such people can have the power to enable, or prevent, the realization of a vision. Being able to influence others' decisions and actions can be critical to eventual success. Those seeking to implement an idea should consider the roles to be played by others, identify others who can expedite the realization of the vision, and determine how to encourage their participation.

The need to maintain flexible plans as one pursues a vision was also a relevant finding of this study. These participants changed their plans and approaches when the need arose or if more promising opportunities presented themselves. They exhibited commitment and dedication to fulfilling their vision.

Based on the findings of this study, individuals wishing to bring their idea to life will find that being committed (*Commitment =Tenacity X Resourcefulness*) will aid in their efforts. Those seeking to implement their visions can anticipate encountering obstacles as they progress from idea to actualization of their creation. Rather than being discouraged by such occurrences, such individuals should not lose heart, but rather find new approaches or modify their expectations in order to achieve their goals.

Participants exhibited a positive attitude and a belief in possibilities. This optimism served them well when they encountered obstacles and setbacks. They weren't dissuaded from achieving their vision and focused on the positive aspects of situations. The participants responded positively to the experience of bringing an idea to fruition. Their reflection on this experience was that it contributed to their confidence and gave them a sense of satisfaction. They took pride in having taken an idea from conception to implementation.

The findings of this study provide insight for those interested in understanding the process of conceiving an idea and following it through to fruition. This study illustrated the linkages between creativity (thinking of something new), motivation (purposeful action, entrepreneurship), and change (transition to something new).

In summary, the participants varied in personality and temperament, but shared many similar characteristics. They were purposeful, visionary, flexible, tenacious, and had a positive attitude. Vision was a central element for the participants in this study, and it served to sustain them throughout the process of implementing their concrete entity.

I've spent several years as an Organization Development (OD) consultant and can see many links between my work, or that of any OD consultant, and the findings of this study. OD practitioners consult with individuals and groups to clarify and create the change they seek. The findings of this study support a basic tenet of the field of OD which states that a powerful vision is an important precursor to change. This study may provide insight as to the processes followed by the participants who were successful in their efforts to implement the change they envisioned. OD practitioners may want to use the themes as a process mapping tool or model to create a framework for groups or individuals seeking to implement ideas.

Also consistent with OD principles, this study supports the need to remain flexible while pursuing goals and to possess the ability to react to and learn from new information as it presents itself. This study provided examples of flexibility from those who were successful in implementing their vision. OD practitioners may find these examples illustrative as they seek to guide others who desire to bring their ideas to life.

Coaching is one of the interventions used by OD practitioners when working with individuals. Coaching is a process of helping individuals assess their current state, articulate their visions, and understand how to develop a path to realize their desired futures. Some findings of this study may provide examples for OD practitioners seeking to coach others. The traits and characteristics identified as key to success for those seeking to bring ideas to fruition could be used as a component of a self-assessment for those interested in entrepreneurial ventures. The processes described in this study may help create an action plan for those seeking to implement their ideas.

OD practitioners work at the individual, team, and organizational level. Understanding the process of moving from idea to implementation at the individual level may be helpful when attempting to understand the process at the group and organizational level. OD consultants may find the themes of this study, which were based on individual experience, provide a template for defining successful processes and necessary traits and characteristics for groups.

Meeting the extraordinary participants in this study and carefully examining their experiences provided valuable learning for me. I have been able to apply my new knowledge from this research not only to enrich my life, but also to enhance the lives of those with whom I interact as a consultant, colleague, and fellow human being.

APPENDIX

RESEARCH METHODOLOGY

A summary of the methodology used in this study is provided for those who are interested in how the data was gathered and analyzed. This was an interpretive, qualitative study, and as such sought to find the meaning of the experience from the subjects' perspective.

Assumptions

An assumption underlying interpretive, qualitative research is that truth is known through experience and defined by those having the experience (Patton, 1990). Qualitative research also assumes that researchers cannot totally separate themselves from the environment in which they are conducting research and that the researchers are the primary instrument for collecting and analyzing data (Miles & Huberman, 1994).

As the researcher, it is necessary that I recognize my own assumptions regarding the phenomenon of taking an idea from conception to fruition. Articulating my assumptions helped me bracket my preconceptions, set them aside, and remain objective when observing and analyzing the experience of the participants in this study. My assumptions regarding the phenomenon being studied before beginning the study were that individuals who see an idea through to implementation must be passionate about the idea and feel driven to implement it. I also assumed that they would develop a plan and that the plan would guide their actions, allowing for inevitable modifications as unexpected obstacles present themselves. I believed the process would be challenging and facing and conquering the challenge would engender a sense of accomplishment. My final assumption was that individuals who are able to bring their ideas to fruition either have the necessary resources to implement their vision, or that these resources are readily available.

This study was based on a number of fundamental assumptions. The first was that individuals who had gone through the experience of moving from idea to implementation could be identified. A second assumption was that an adequate number of such individuals would be willing to participate in this study. Another assumption was that those who brought an idea to completion could reflect on and describe how their initial idea surfaced, what caused them to pursue the idea, the process they used to bring the idea to fruition, and what meaning the experience has had for them.

Research Design and Methodology

This study used an interpretive epistemological approach and followed a basic qualitative study design. This approach was appropriate for the study because interpretivism is based on the belief that reality is socially constructed and can only be understood in the context in which it occurs. Interpretivists are not seeking generalizable truth but rather seek to understand the truth as it is known to the participants in the study, in their own environment (Patton, 1990). In an interpretive study, the knowledge gained is the understanding of the meaning of the experience through an inductive form of inquiry (Merriam, 1998).

My goal was consistent with the interpretive epistemology in that I was seeking to understand the participants' experience of moving from the inception of an idea to the implementation of that idea from their perspective, the process in which they engaged, and their traits and characteristics. Further, I wanted to determine whether there were commonalities of experience across the group of participants. My study fit the criteria Merriam provided for a basic qualitative study because it was the study of a process, and sought to understand the phenomenon of moving from ideation to implementation through the perspective of the participants.

Data was collected through basic qualitative study methods of interviews, observations and document analysis. Analysis of the data allowed me to identify recurring patterns. The results of the study include description and analysis, and explore a process. A basic qualitative study was an appropriate methodology for this study because it provided a framework that allowed exploration of a complex phenomenon from the perspective of those experiencing it.

Sampling

Participants for this study were selected using purposeful sampling. Purposeful sampling allows for the selection of information-rich participants (Patton, 1990). It is based on the assumption that the researcher wants to gain insight and therefore must purposefully select participants from whom the researcher can learn the most (Merriam, 1998). Purposeful sampling defines the limits of the universe in which the participants will be found and usually results in a relatively small sample size of participants who are nested in their context and studied in depth (Miles & Huberman, 1994).

It was important to study the phenomenon as it became evident in a variety of settings, and not just how it revealed itself under specific conditions. Purposeful sampling provides for selecting participants from an array of settings, thus increasing the variability of the sample (Maykut & Morehouse, 1994). Including participants from different venues focused the study on the actual process of moving from idea to implementation and did not confine it to how that process unfolded in any particular setting.

I included only those who had taken an idea to fruition, since only they could answer the key questions of this study based on their personal experience. The common denominator for the participants in this study was having had a thought about creating something and then following through to see their idea implemented or realized.

Participant Identification

The participants were identified through (1) my own knowledge of their having brought an idea into reality; (2) colleagues or acquaintances telling me of someone they knew who had done so; and (3) working backwards by identifying something that was in existence and determining who had the original idea to create it. It was not difficult to find potential participants for this study.

The greater challenge was determining the type of participant diversity I wanted to achieve. I determined that the sector or domain (e.g., business, education, community service) in which the individual operated would be a primary criterion for deciding who should be invited to participate in the study. In selecting participants, I sought individuals from different sectors to ensure that the phenomenon being studied was not overly influenced by the venue in which it occurred. I was able to identify individuals who had implemented ideas in various venues, including for-profit business, education, non-profit local community services, international humanitarian programs and a faith community.

The participants were also diverse regarding location, education, and gender. This additional diversity in participants further ensured that the phenomenon studied was not the result of a specific demographic of the group studied. I included participants from Minnesota, Florida and Colorado. Minnesota is my home location. I traveled to Florida and Colorado so interviews with individuals in these locations could be conducted in person.

Participant Selection

I made an initial contact with potential participants by in-person meetings, phone calls, emails, or regular mail to tell them about the study and to determine their willingness to participate. I also evaluated whether they met the criteria developed for inclusion in this study, i.e., that the person's idea involved something outside of themselves, was intended to be enduring, and resulted in something tangible and concrete. Another requirement for inclusion in this study was agreeing to audio tape record our interviews.

In a qualitative study such as this, it is difficult to determine the actual number of participants needed before beginning the study. The goal was to have enough participants to adequately answer the key questions of the study. I added participants until I found that the information I gathered was repetitive, and I had participants from enough different venues that my findings were not overly influenced by the sector in which the participants operated. Although each individual's story was unique, patterns emerged as I proceeded through the study. Evident patterns became apparent after four participants were interviewed, but I continued with more interviews to ensure the patterns would be consistent across sectors. These additional interviews also increased the diversity of the participants and the type of ideas included in this study.

Of the eleven incidents of moving from ideation to implementation included in this study, four involved more than one individual who participated in the creation of the idea. In one case business partners jointly developed the idea. In three other situations married couples worked collaboratively to develop and implement their idea. In such cases, I included both individuals in the study; however, together they were considered as one incident of the phenomenon of going from idea to implementation.

Participant Demographics

There are 15 individuals, which represent 11 incidents of going from an idea to implementation in this study. Six of the incidents of the phenomenon explored in this study occurred in Minnesota, three were in Florida and two in Colorado. The participants' level of education ranged from high school graduation to advanced degrees, with the majority of participants having earned Master's degrees.

The age at which the idea originally came to the individuals ranged from childhood to mature adulthood. The majority of participants were mature adults (age 51 or older) both at the time of the interview and when they initially had the idea that they brought to fruition. Six of the 15 individuals represented by the eleven incidents were women. Three of these women partnered with their husbands in bringing their idea into reality and three worked individually. All but one of the participants was Caucasian.

Data Collection Methods

The most frequently used data collection methods in a qualitative study are interviews, observations and document analysis (Merriam, 1998). All three methods were used in this study. Interviewing allows one to find out what is on the participant's mind (Patton, 1990). Observation allows the researcher to collect descriptive data about the setting, people, activities, and meaning from the participant's perspective (Patton, 1990). Reviewing primary and secondary documents can add richness to a qualitative study. Documents that were not created for the research purpose can contain clues or startling insights to the phenomenon being studied (Merriam).

I prepared for each interview by reviewing all the information I had gathered about the individual and the entity they created, while, at the same time, bracketing any assumptions I held about that individual or the entity they created. In bracketing my assumptions I set aside my biases, prejudices, theories, philosophies, even common sense to accept the phenomenon for what it was (Boeree, 1998). As is true of all qualitative researchers, it was important for me to understand my beliefs and biases, so I could successfully navigate the challenge of being both an active instrument in the research process while objectively studying the phenomenon from the participants' perspectives. All of the interviews were conducted face-to-face and generally lasted about an hour and a half. I had follow up phone conversations with several of the participants.

I prepared a structured interview guide that listed specific questions that were to be asked of all participants. These questions helped focus the interview and elicit responses that would shed light on the questions of this study, and provide me with information regarding their experience of moving from idea to implementation. I complemented the use of a structured interview guide with an in-depth, conversational style during the interview. In-depth conversational interviewing was an appropriate methodology for this study because it allowed the individuals to express what was real for them. It did not force an arbitrary measurement or require comparison to some standard, but rather allowed for the exploration of reality as experienced by the individuals who were the participants of this study.

Prior to conducting any interviews, I asked five colleagues to review the interview guide to get their evaluation of whether the questions I prepared were likely to elicit the information I was seeking. The feedback I received on the interview guide was favorable. Those who reviewed it offered a few suggestions for changing individual words and for combining questions to align with the research questions of my study. I incorporated these changes into the interview guide and shared the final form with two of these individuals. Both concurred with the content of the final document.

At the end of each interview, I asked the participants to provide any additional data that they believed would help me understand their journey from idea to implementation. Several participants provided documents such as copies of books they had written, personal notes, materials describing the entity they created, and articles written by others.

In some instances, I was able to interview those who had been in a position to observe and interact with the participants during the process of bringing their idea to fruition. I asked these individuals for their perception of how the participant moved from idea to implementation, and their assessment of the participant's characteristics and traits. Comments from those who had the opportunity to observe the process of bringing the idea to implementation provided additional insight into understanding the process and the individuals involved. I either taped these interviews or took extensive notes. This additional information was subsequently transcribed and I reviewed the transcriptions or my typed notes from these interviews as part of my analysis of the data.

I researched the accomplishments of the participants from other sources, such as journals, newspapers, business reports, magazine articles, and internet resources. Examining documents and artifacts associated with these individuals' achievements provided another perspective for the study. When possible, I observed the entity they created. In seven cases, I was able to watch the participants as they worked in this entity. I was given tours of six of the establishments and visited some on my own. I observed the physical and cultural aspects of the entity and talked with other workers and customers at these facilities. These visits helped me substantiate that the idea the participants created met the criteria of being enduring, sustainable, concrete and tangible. I recorded my observations of the entities created and reviewed these notes as part of my data analysis.

Data Analysis

To help address the potential conflict of researcher bias, I used a constant comparative method (Patton, 1990) to analyze the data. The constant comparison method involves constantly comparing data with the goal of identifying patterns that allow the data to be separated into themes (Patton, 1990). When practicing constant comparison, one of the first tasks is to gather data bits into temporary categories (Lincoln & Guba, 1985). Dey, Schatz, Rosenberg, & Coleman (2000) use the metaphor of a kaleidoscope to describe constant comparison. In this metaphor, the small bits of neon glass represent data bits that churn to form a variety of patterns. Whereas devising categories is predominately an intuitive process, it is also systematic and informed by the purpose of the study, the researcher's knowledge, and the meaning made explicit by the participants (Merriam, 1998).

I thoroughly studied all the data I gathered on each participant. I carefully read each interview transcript to be able to summarize the experience of moving from idea to implementation from each participant's perspective. I read the transcripts as they were completed in sequence. I developed a coding system to help sort the data into themes. After reviewing the transcript from the first interview, I did an initial coding of the participant's comments to start identifying potential themes. I also reviewed all the other information I was able to gather about the participant and did an initial coding on the parts of these documents that were relevant to my study.

After the second interview, I repeated the process of coding potential themes. I then reviewed my coding and notes from the first interview, comparing them to the second and identified those data elements that were similar and those that were unique. I repeated the same process after each interview.

The theme titles evolved through an iterative process. Consistent with the process described by Maykut and

Morehouse (1994), I accepted patterns as tentative and was willing to reconstruct these patterns when confronted with new patterns that emerged from the study to "let the data speak for itself" (p. 35). I completed a thematic analysis of the interview transcriptions and other documents by looking for recurring words and phrases that indicated shared experiences. I revised the categories into which the data bits were sorted several times throughout my analysis.

I developed a list of the preliminary themes that emerged from the data. I created tables that listed these preliminary themes and recorded evidence, such as a quotation from an interview or other source, for each incidence of the phenomenon in this study that supported the preliminary theme. This method provided another way to validate that the themes I saw emerging from the data were evident for all cases in this study. I followed the same process with data I collected about Sona Mehring, who was added as a participant after the completion of my dissertation.

To help ensure that my conclusions from the data were valid, I had five colleagues review the interview transcripts and asked them to independently identify the themes they saw emerging from the data. Each person reviewed at least two of the transcripts. There was consistency between the preliminary themes I identified and those identified by my colleagues.

I shared definitions used in this study and a summary of my findings and analysis with the participants. I provided each with a copy of the preliminary findings that described their experiences. I asked that they review the information for accuracy and tell me if any changes were required. I also asked that they indicate whether or not they agreed with the conclusions I drew, thus using a "member check" method to help validate my findings. The purpose of the member check was not only to test the factual and interpretive accuracy of what was reported, but also to provide evidence of credibility (Lincoln & Guba, 1985).

The participants' response to this inquiry was voluntary and not a precondition of participation in the study. However, all of the participants responded. All indicated that they supported my analysis. Some offered a few corrections of titles and details in the stories, but no one expressed disagreement with the themes I identified or offered any major revisions to the information included about themselves. Several indicated that they were pleased to be part of the study.

REFERENCES

Ball, J. (2002, February). Saints and heroes among us. *Everyday Catholic*. Retrieved January 24, 2005, from http://www.amoeicancatholic.org/newsletter/EDC/ag0202.asp.

Boeree, C. G. (1998). *Qualitative methods.* Retrieved January 21, 2006, from http://www.ship.edu%Ecghoeree/qualimethone.html.

Cayla, J. (2013, September). Next! Leslie Lascheid Takes the Reins. *Gulfshore Life.*

Covey, S. (2004). *The 7 habits of highly effective people: Powerful lessons in personal change.* New York, NY: Simon and Schuster.

Csikszentmihalyi, Mihaly. (1996). *Creativity: Flow and the psychology of discovery and invention.* New York, NY. Harper Perennial.

Dey, J. F., Schatz, I. M., Rosenberg, B. A., & Coleman, S. T. (2000). Constant comparison method: A kaleidoscope of data. *The Qualitative Report*, 4(2). Retrieved February 7, 2005, from http://www.nova.edu/ssss/QR/QR4-1/dye.html.

Graham, R. (2011, August). CaringBridge's Sona Mehring On Being The One Woman In the Room. *The Grindstone*

Executive Suite: Retrieved August 16, 2013 from http://www.thegrindstone.com/2011/08/23/mentors/executive-suite.

Kouze, J. & Posner, B). (2013). 5th ed. *The leadership challenge how to make extraordinary things happen in organizations.* San Francisco, CA: Jossey-Bass.

Lincoln, Y & Guba, M. (1985). *Naturalistic Inquiry.* Newbury Park, CA: Sage.

Maykut, P., & Morehouse, R. (1994). *Beginning qualitative research: A philosophic and practical guide.* Washington, D. C.: The Father Press.

Mehring, S (2010, May). *Harnessing the Internet for Hope and Support.* Retrieved August 13, 2013 from http://kriscarr.com/blog.

Merriam, S. (1998). *Qualitative research and case study applications in education.* San Francisco: CA Jossey-Bass.

Merriam – Webster's Collegiate Dictionary. (2004). 11th Ed. Springfield, MS: Merrriam-Webster, Inc.

Miles, M. B., & Huberman, A. M. (1994). *An expanded sourcebook: Qualitative data analysis.* Thousand Oaks, CA: Sage Publications.

Norwood, J. (1996). KidzArt: A private approach to serving at-risk youth. *Better Government Competition,* Cascade Policy Institute.

Patton, M. (1990). *Qualitative evaluation methods.* (Rev. ed.). Thousand Oaks, CA: Sage Publications.

Sparks, L, (2004, August). The plentiful harvest: How one couple's vision is changing Immokalee's future. *Gulf Coast Business Community.* Pg. 6-7.

Stanley, C. (2013, September). Next! Leslie Lascheid Takes the Reins.*Gulfshore Life.*

ABOUT THE AUTHOR

Dr. Diane J. Hinds graduated with a bachelor's degree in psychology and communication before going on to earn her master's in human resources development and a doctorate in organization development.

The owner of Achieve, a consulting and training company that helps both individuals and organizations achieve their goals, Hinds has over thirty years experience in human resources, organization development and executive level management.